WHY THE TITANIC WAS DOOMED

WHY THE TITANIC WAS DOOMED

A DISASTER OF CIRCUMSTANCE

BRYAN JACKSON

PEN & SWORD
HISTORY

AN IMPRINT OF PEN & SWORD BOOKS LTD.
YORKSHIRE – PHILADELPHIA

First published in Great Britain in 2022 by
PEN AND SWORD HISTORY
An imprint of
Pen & Sword Books Ltd
Yorkshire – Philadelphia

ISBN 978 1 39909 716 1

Typeset in Times New Roman 12/16 by SJmagic DESIGN SERVICES, India.
Printed and bound in the UK by CPI Group (UK) Ltd.

Pen & Sword Books Limited incorporates the imprints of Atlas, Archaeology,
Aviation, Discovery, Family History, Fiction, History, Maritime, Military, Military
Classics, Politics, Select, Transport, True Crime, Air World, Frontline Publishing,
Leo Cooper, Remember When, Seaforth Publishing, The Praetorian Press,
Wharncliffe Local History, Wharncliffe Transport, Wharncliffe True Crime and
White Owl.

For a complete list of Pen & Sword titles please contact
PEN & SWORD BOOKS LIMITED
47 Church Street, Barnsley, South Yorkshire, S70 2AS, England
E-mail: enquiries@pen-and-sword.co.uk
Website: www.pen-and-sword.co.uk

Or

PEN AND SWORD BOOKS
1950 Lawrence Rd, Havertown, PA 19083, USA
E-mail: Uspen-and-sword@casematepublishers.com
Website: www.penandswordbooks.com

Contents

Preface

It is an understatement to say that much has been written about one of the world's most famous ships, *Titanic*. Within days of her sinking, books, articles and movies about the disaster started to appear and be consumed by a public anxious to learn everything it could about the loss of the great liner, and those that had sailed in her.

By the middle of the twentieth century, *Titanic* was again capturing the public's attention with the release of *Titanic* in 1953, a dramatic adaptation of the sinking starring Barbara Stanwyck. It would soon be followed by the historical retelling of the disaster in Walter Lord's book *A Night to Remember*. By 1958, Lord's book had been turned into a movie with the same name.

A vast new collection of *Titanic* books, documentaries and news items were again spurred by her discovery on the ocean floor in 1985 by a joint French-American expedition led by Jean-Louis Michel and Robert Ballard – along with a new generation of enthusiasts that some have come to call 'Titaniacs'.

The technology that had allowed man to reach *Titanic* two miles below the surface of the North Atlantic also brought an in-depth exploration of her remains, along with new theories and research as to what caused her untimely loss. These developments would once again renew interest in the liner that was once the pride of the White Star Line.

Within a decade, it would even lead to another movie named *Titanic*, this time with Hollywood grafting a fabricated love story onto the disaster. Despite its interjection of the fictional passengers Jack and Rose, *Titanic* once again grabbed the attention of yet another generation, who otherwise likely would never have heard of the ship or the tragedy that befell her.

Of course, the centennial of her sinking in April 2012 provided *Titanic* enthusiasts, researchers and the media with the perfect opportunity to yet again revisit and discuss her story – along with the production of another round of articles, books, videos and commemorative items.

So although *Titanic* may fade from view for a while, she always returns because her story is one that cannot be forgotten – and the lessons she taught cannot be ignored. Not now, not ever.

As for myself, I clearly remember my first introduction to *Titanic* many years ago. I was in seventh grade and I was required to write a book report for English class. As a kid, I was not a big reader – so being assigned a book report was nothing short of pure drudgery.

My task was to pick a book from the school library or select a title from a list of books we could buy. The library held nothing of interest to me, but there was a title on the list of books for sale that caught my eye – *A Night to Remember* by Walter Lord. The brief description hooked me immediately: a mighty ship that struck an iceberg and sank on its maiden voyage with a great loss of life. I dug out the 50 cents it cost and proceeded to devour its pages in one sitting. *Titanic* has kept my attention ever since – and I still have my copy of Lord's excellent work, though its pages are faded and frayed from the countless times I have read it.

Over the years, I have tried to consume each new book, article and documentary about *Titanic*. But it has occurred to me that one perspective always seemed to be missing – the many circumstances, large and small, that came together to doom the ship that many had considered unsinkable. I found many of those facts and much of that information scattered piecemeal elsewhere, but I had never found it all brought together into a single work that would show that her eventual fate was much more than just an unfortunate accident.

Preface

In preparing this book, I found myself discovering new information and rethinking some of what I thought I knew about *Titanic* and the circumstances leading to her loss. I hope you find this collection of information enlightening too.

And, if you ever have to do a book report on this book, I hope you find this one worthy of a favourable review.

Acknowledgements

While I have written thousands of news stories and press releases during my career in journalism and public relations, this was my first venture into book publishing.

Although I spent the better part of two years working on this book, it might still be languishing unpublished if it were not for my life-long friend, Floyd Vivino. Known to many as the comedian 'Uncle Floyd', he is also a history buff and he asked to read what I had written about the *Titanic*. Two days after he received my manuscript, he was on the phone to tell me that he found it fascinating, adding that he could not put it down. He urged me to find a publisher – and so I owe him a big debt of gratitude for giving me the confidence to move forward.

I fully expected finding a reputable and interested publisher would be a long, arduous journey. I did some quick online research and soon found Pen and Sword. It seemed like a good match, so I sent a copy of the manuscript to Jonathan Wright, who handles its acquisitions, and was pleasantly surprised when I received an immediate response of interest. A few emails later, we had an agreement to move forward. Jon has been an amazing partner and I cannot thank him enough for his support and assistance.

Thanks also goes to Michelle Higgs, who worked with me on proofing and editing the book. Her keen eye and true interest ensured that nothing was overlooked. I was particularly impressed with her incredible attention to detail. Although I had pored over my manuscript countless times, she still found items that needed to be double-checked and corrected, as well as recommendations for worthy improvements to the text. Michelle proved the old adage that you can never accurately proof your own work.

Acknowledgements

Guiding production of this book were Pen and Sword's Charlotte Mitchell and Laura Hirst. Their direction and assistance were invaluable and very much appreciated.

Although they are long deceased, there are two people I also want to acknowledge, as their work has allowed us to peer into *Titanic*'s brief existence. The first is Robert Welch, Harland & Wolff's official photographer. He meticulously documented every step of the great liner's construction and launch – and many of his photos are included in this book.

The other is Reverend Francis Patrick Browne, a distinguished Irish Jesuit priest and a prolific photographer. He sailed aboard *Titanic* on her maiden voyage, travelling from Southampton to Queenstown. During his short day-and-a-half trip, he took dozens of photographs. They included pictures of the gymnasium, the radio room, the first-class dining saloon, his own cabin, and passengers walking along the promenade and boat decks. He captured the last known images of many crew-members and passengers – and took the last known image of *Titanic* as she departed Ireland for New York. It is featured on the cover of this book.

Of course, I would be remiss if I did not thank my wife, Nora. Her encouragement kept me going – although I suspect some of it was for her own benefit. I am sure she wanted the book finished so she could regain use of our dining room table, which had become my 'office' during the project.

Now I need to write another book – if for no other reason than to be able to work with this great group of people once again. Thank you all.

Finally, thanks to you – my readers. Your interest in *Titanic* will forever keep her memory alive.

Introduction

Ask someone what caused the *Titanic* to sink and they will tell you, 'It hit an iceberg.' In fact, the man who led the expedition that found the *Titanic* during the summer of 1985, Dr Robert Ballard, put it even more bluntly when he said: 'It hit an iceberg and it sank. Get over it.'

Yet, while that's the simple answer, there is much more to it. Circumstances had lined up to doom the *Titanic* before it ever left the shipyard. In fact, even before she had left the drawing board.

Like an iceberg itself, most of what preceded the world's best known maritime disaster lies mostly under the surface. In fact, if any one of the circumstances behind the tragedy had not happened, *Titanic* and the iceberg might never have crossed paths, leaving the great ship to be long forgotten like so many other first-rate transatlantic liners of its era.

But *Titanic* – and over 1,500 of her passengers – were all doomed long before she departed Southampton on her maiden voyage. The circumstances of her loss – and the deaths of so many aboard her – ranged from design flaws to errors in judgement by men with just seconds to make decisions. Even her own sister ship, *Olympic* (ironically nicknamed '*Old Reliable*'), would play a major role in *Titanic*'s destruction.

Each was a circumstance that alone might not have mattered much. But when added together, they combined to destroy the most luxurious passenger ship ever built.

This is the story of how those circumstances came together in the North Atlantic on the freezing cold night of 14 April 1912.

The First Circumstance
A Delayed Maiden Voyage

The *Titanic* was the second of three great sister ships of the White Star Line, with the *Olympic* being built, launched and put into service first in 1911. *Titanic* and *Britannic* would follow. Each one was just over 882 feet long, making them the largest man-made moving objects of their time.

Olympic's construction would begin in December 1909, three months before *Titanic*'s keel would be laid. The staggered schedule was to ease the workload on Harland & Wolff, the Belfast shipyard hired by White Star to build its extraordinary liners.

Olympic would begin her sea trials on 29 May 1911 and then leave the shipyard on 31 May, bound for Liverpool, her port of registration. To gain publicity for its new luxury liners, the White Star Line decided to set the start of *Olympic*'s first trip to coincide with the launch day of her sister, *Titanic*. The stunt garnered worldwide attention for these mammoth new ships. And many newspapers used the opportunity to perpetuate the myth begun earlier when *Shipbuilder* magazine published a story stating that these new liners were 'practically unsinkable.' Within a short time after that article appeared, the word 'practically' would lose its place in almost all of the stories that followed elsewhere.

After arriving in Liverpool, *Olympic* spent a day giving members of the public an opportunity to come on board and tour the magnificent ship and its lavish appointments. Next, she sailed to Southampton, arriving on 3 June at the deep-water dock that had been specially constructed to accommodate these new '*Olympic*-class' liners.

The new 'White Star Dock' was near the company's headquarters, which itself sat on the Southampton waterfront.

Olympic's maiden voyage began on 14 June 1911, sailing from Southampton to Cherbourg, France, and then to Queenstown, Ireland (now Cobb) – the same route that *Titanic* would take the following year. She would reach New York on 21 June with Captain Edward Smith at the helm. Smith, considered the most seasoned of the White Star's captains, would also command the *Titanic* on her maiden voyage. But the result would be very different – and cost him his life.

In New York, as in Liverpool, the *Olympic* was opened to the public for a day while docked along the Manhattan shoreline. Over 8,000 curious visitors came aboard to marvel at this ocean-going technological feat. Another 10,000 would show up to watch her depart for her return trip to England a few days later.

In the beginning, *Olympic*'s Atlantic crossings would become almost a matter of routine – until her fifth voyage.

On 20 September 1911, just after *Olympic* had left Southampton, she collided with the British cruiser HMS *Hawke* while both were steaming off the Isle of Wight. The two ships had been running parallel to each other when the *Olympic* began to turn to starboard. The wide turn surprised the captain of the *Hawke*, who was unable to manoeuvre his ship in time to avoid colliding with the stern of the great superliner. Adding to the accident was the fact that no one really understood the physical dynamics of these giant new ships or the suction they created as they moved through the water. Despite the *Hawke*'s desperate attempt to avoid the collision, she could not overcome being sucked into the stern of *Olympic*'s starboard side as water rushed to fill the void left by the bigger ship's wake.

The *Hawke*'s bow, which was reinforced and designed for ramming other ships in combat, sliced into *Olympic*'s hull, tearing large holes in her right side and flooding two of her aft watertight compartments. In addition to the hull damage, the crash bent the *Olympic*'s starboard propeller shaft.

Miraculously, both ships survived, although the *Hawke*'s damaged bow nearly caused her to capsize. *Olympic*'s crew was able to stabilise the ship and safely return under her own power to Southampton. There she was temporarily patched up before leaving for Belfast for permanent repairs.

Although there were no injuries or deaths in the collision, the incident received widespread attention and produced an unintended consequence. The fact that the *Olympic* had endured such a serious collision and stayed afloat lent credence to the belief that the design of these new *Olympic*-class liners had indeed made them 'unsinkable.'

Once back in Belfast, it took just over a month and a half to repair the damaged *Olympic*. To get her back in service faster, parts and labour were diverted from the *Titanic*, which was still under construction at the Harland & Wolff shipyard. This included taking the starboard propeller shaft from the *Titanic* to replace the one damaged by the *Hawke*.

The *Titanic* would again help her sister ship in February 1912 when *Olympic* lost a propeller blade while returning to Southampton from New York. As before, *Olympic* limped back to Belfast for repairs, with resources being diverted to her from the *Titanic*.

As a result of *Olympic*'s misfortunes, *Titanic*'s maiden voyage would be postponed from 20 March 1912 to 10 April 1912 – and this change of date would seal *Titanic*'s fate.

According to reports from 1912, very little ice had strayed down into the North Atlantic shipping lanes before April. But by the second week of that month, numerous radio reports of hazardous ice had begun to come in:

6 April – British Steamer *Strathfillan* reports latitude 49 N 48 W, encountered ice;

3 April – Danish steamer [name unreadable] latitude 45 04 N, longitude 56 38 W saw drifting ice and ice fields;

7 April – The *Armenian* reports latitude 42 36 N longitude 49 36 W, encountered field ice which extended for a distance of 50 miles;

7 April – British Steamer *Rosalind* ran into a strip of field ice 3 or 4 miles wide, extending north and south as far as could be seen in 45 10 N 56 40 W;

8 April – British Steamer *Brinkburn* reports latitude 47 longitude 47, encountered ice, field ice and numerous small bergs;

8 April – British Steamer *Lord Cromer* at 150 miles east of St. Johns, Newfoundland encountered much field ice;

8 April – British Steamer *Royal Edwards* reports from 42 5 N 49 39 W to 42 30 N 50 10 W, passed thick and heavy loose field ice. At 42 48N 49 40W, saw a large iceberg;

8 April – British Steamer *Rio Pirahy* reports in latitude 42 44 longitude 49 34, for 7 hours passed a large quantity of field ice and icebergs;

9 April – The *Knutsford*, on route from New York, reports a temperature drop in 40 56 N 47 56 W which was attributed to a huge iceberg seen 1.5 hours later.

Before these dates – and especially along the New York route that *Titanic* would travel – the shipping lanes had remained mostly clear of ice and safe. This leaves little doubt that had *Titanic* left Southampton on 20 March as originally planned, she would have likely travelled to New York without encountering the danger presented by icebergs. But the delay of her maiden voyage would change all that, allowing the Labrador Current to push the Arctic's lethal ice farther south.

By the night of 14 April 1912, the current would place a deadly iceberg directly in front of *Titanic*.

The Second Circumstance
The Near Miss that Almost Ended the Deadly Maiden Voyage

As *Titanic* set sail on 10 April 1912, it had one more 'opportunity' that might have kept her from the fatal encounter with the iceberg four days later.

As she pulled away from Berth 44, Southampton's docks were littered with ships that had been idled by the national coal strike which had crippled England. The strike had begun in February and lasted until early April, but the supply lines that transported the coal to its end-users were still empty and it would take weeks before things were back to normal.

Titanic had only managed to keep her scheduled sailing date because she had pillaged coal – and many passengers – from no less than five other ships operated by lines controlled by the International Mercantile Marine conglomerate, which included the White Star, Red Star and the American Lines. Among them was the *New York,* which lay tied up at the end of the Southampton dock complex on the River Test.

Although Captain Edward Smith, the Commodore of the White Star Line, had been chosen to command *Titanic* on her maiden voyage, Harbour Pilot George Bowyer was on the bridge guiding her away from the dock and out into open waters. Bowyer had also been in charge of the *Olympic* when she turned in front of the British warship *Hawke* and was pierced by her bow, taking both ships out of service for weeks. Now it appeared Bowyer and *Titanic* were about to do an encore.

As *Titanic* slid past the idled *New York*, the new pride of the White Star Line was simply travelling much too fast. Her great hull created a powerful suction as the water she displaced rushed back in to fill the void where she had been. The force pulled hard against the smaller *New York* and soon the forces were too much for her mooring lines. A series of sharp 'bangs' – sounding much like gunshots – pierced the air as *New York*'s hawsers snapped as though they were pieces of twine.

With nothing to hold her in place, the *New York* swung out with the suction pulling her directly towards *Titanic*. For many anxious moments it seemed that a collision was inevitable – and that *Titanic*'s maiden voyage would end just minutes after it had started. Her passengers, and the many hundreds of onlookers on shore who had come to see her off, could only watch as the pending accident unfolded before them.

As the *New York* continued to draw near, *Titanic*'s Third Officer, Herbert Pitman, picked up his megaphone and shouted from the aft docking bridge that the port propeller should be put full ahead to create a wash that would push the ever-encroaching ship away. Bowyer quickly rang the order on the engine room telegraph, and the *New York* finally stopped her unrelenting advance. Two nearby tugs raced to the side of the drifting orphan and were able to pull her away to safety. The *New York* and the *Titanic* had been only inches away from each other before the disaster was averted.

Had the two ships collided, *Titanic*'s maiden voyage would have almost certainly been delayed, as she would have likely been pulled from service to undergo repairs – just as *Olympic* had been the year before. This change in circumstances might very well have also changed the fate of *Titanic*, keeping her from being in the wrong place at the wrong time just four days later.

The Third Circumstance
Telegrams that Could Have
Changed History

There can be no doubt that the captain and crew of the *Titanic* knew there was dangerous ice ahead of them. On 11 April, just three days before the *Titanic* disaster, SS *Niagara* had struck two icebergs less than 10 miles from where *Titanic* would meet her eventual end. The bergs punched two holes in the *Niagara*'s hull below the waterline, but she was able to survive thanks to pumps which kept ahead of the inrushing water.

On the night of 14 April – the same night the *Titanic* struck the iceberg – the Cunard liner *Carmania* arrived in New York with Captain Daniel Dow remarking, 'I have never seen ice so far south.' In his logbook he recorded that his ship had to skirt a vast ice field during the afternoon of 11 April – with some icebergs towering an estimated 400 feet high. He also noted that his ship had been called by the *Niagara* to come and lend assistance after she struck ice, but that he was able to finally resume his original route to New York after the stricken ship radioed that she had the damage under control and was out of danger.

Throughout the day on 14 April, the airwaves continued to crackle with ice warnings. They began that Sunday morning around 9.00 am with a message from the *Caronia* which radioed:

> Bergs, growlers, and field ice in 42 degrees North from
> 49 to 51 degrees West.

At 11.20 am, the *Amerika* followed, asking *Titanic* to relay a warning that it had seen two large icebergs in the vicinity of 41 degrees 27 minutes North and 50 degrees 8 minutes West. That message pinpointed almost the exact spot where *Titanic* would eventually collide with deadly ice just 12 hours later.

At 11.40 am another warning was received – this time from the *Noordam*. Its brief but direct message was, 'Much ice.' A few minutes later, the White Star's *Baltic* hailed her fleet mate *Titanic* to announce: 'Icebergs and large quantities of field ice in 41 degrees North to 51 degrees North, 49 degrees to 52 degrees West.'

Baltic concluded her message with: 'Wish you and *Titanic* all success.'

Even some of *Titanic*'s passengers knew first-hand of the ice warnings, as the *Baltic*'s message was later shared with a group of them by White Star President, Bruce Ismay. They included first-class passenger Emily Ryerson, who said Ismay approached her as she stood on the promenade watching the sunset. In a letter she wrote on 18 April 1913 – just over a year after the ship sank in the Atlantic Ocean – she recalled their meeting:

> Mr. Ismay thrusts a Marconigram at me saying we were in among the icebergs. They were to start up extra boilers that afternoon. My impression was that they were speeding the ship up to get away from the ice, and that we would probably get in late Tuesday night or early Wednesday morning.

Her letter would also tacitly implicate Ismay in causing the disaster:

> Mr. Ismay's manner was that of one in authority and the owner of the ship and that what he said was law. If this can be of service to anyone, I do not wish to be silent to seem to be protecting him.

Despite what was contained in her letter, Ryerson never pointed the finger of blame at Ismay during the testimony she gave to the official inquiries that followed *Titanic*'s loss.

After Ismay had shown the *Baltic*'s warning to several others, Captain Smith asked for it to be returned so it could be posted in the ship's chart-room.

Later that evening, around 7.50 pm, *Titanic* received one of its most important ice warnings from the Atlantic Transport Line steamer MV *Mesaba*. But the warning apparently never left the radio room, although it read:

> In lat 42N to 41.25N long 49W to long 50.30W saw much heavy pack ice and great number of large icebergs, also field ice. Weather good, clear.

The master of the *Mesaba* would later write in the ship's log that he was forced to change course and sail south 20 miles because of the wall of ice his ship encountered. It would take two hours before he was able to turn westward once again, free of the ice that had blocked his path.

Although the *Mesaba*'s telegram gave *Titanic* clear and precise details of the enormous ice field that lay directly in her path, the surviving officers of the *Titanic* later testified at a U.S. Senate hearing that they never saw the message. Their consensus was that the ship would have slowed or changed course – *if* the crew had been aware of the warning.

There have been a number of theories as to the circumstances that resulted in this message never leaving the radio room.

Perhaps the most damning is that it was not sent with the all-important '*MSG*' or *Master Service Gram* designation – an indication that it was a personal message to the *Titanic*'s captain. Under regulations in effect at that time, all such messages were required to be delivered to the ship's master, who, in turn, was required to acknowledge it had been received. Without the '*MSG*' prefix, the radio room was under no legal obligation to send it to the bridge. The message was likely shoved aside after it was received.

Still, every ship travelling along this North Atlantic route – including *Titanic* – knew it had become hazardous. Indeed, very hazardous.

***

Earlier in the day the German-flagged SS *Amerika* sent an ice warning while also headed eastbound to the United States, steaming ahead of *Titanic*. When the *Amerika* entered a large field of icebergs, her captain ordered his radio operator, Otto Reuter, to send their location to the Hydrographic Office in Washington, DC.

Radio equipment in 1912 was still quite primitive, and the *Amerika*'s gear was not as powerful as those of newer ships like the *Titanic*. And because its transmitter and antenna were not strong enough to reach the distant station at Cape Race on the coast of Newfoundland, the *Amerika* engaged in the then-common practice of asking for its ice warning to be relayed by a ship with a more powerful radio set. In this case the request was made of *Titanic*.

The relay carried the following message:

> SS *Amerika* via SS *Titanic* and Cape Race N.E 14 April 1912
>
> Hydrographic Office, Washington DC
>
> *Amerika* passed two large icebergs in 41 27N 50.8 W on the 14th of April
>
> Knupt (sic), 10;51p

When the *Amerika*'s request to relay its ice warning came in, *Titanic*'s chief radio operator, Jack Phillips, sent it and then likely 'spiked' it onto the pile of completed messages. Because it was considered a relay message – not one specifically directed to *Titanic* herself – Phillips would have considered the task complete. However, the relay meant that *Titanic* not only knew the exact location of the iceberg that would cause her destruction, but that she had ironically sent that very warning herself to the Hydrographic Office and other ships as well.

***

Then, just a few hours before the tragedy, another event took place that kept some ice warnings from getting to the *Titanic*'s bridge.

Although *Titanic* boasted the latest in radio technology, her wireless set was still primitive and could be unreliable. On 13 April – the day before *Titanic* struck the iceberg – the Marconi wireless set malfunctioned and stopped operating.

Under the company's rules, a less powerful backup set was to be used and repairs of the main set were to be left to service personnel once the ship reached its destination. But this would leave *Titanic*'s two radio operators, Jack Phillips and his assistant, Harold Bride, with far less ability to reach the distant land-based wireless stations needed to relay messages from the ship to their eventual recipients across the United States and Canada.

Frustrated, Phillips decided to ignore the company's instructions and attempt to fix the main set instead. Diagnosing and repairing the broken equipment would take time, and hours passed as the two men patiently dug through the guts of the transmitter, carefully inspecting each section in an effort to locate the problem. Finally, in a stroke of rare good luck that evening, faulty wiring in a transformer was found and repaired.

Little did they know that their diligence would allow them to call for help – and save hundreds of lives – just a few hours later.

As they had struggled to fix the radio, *Titanic*'s passengers – among them some of the world's wealthiest individuals – had continued to inundate the radio room with messages. Radiograms from sea were an exciting new miracle and the wealthy on board this maiden voyage delighted in sending them to family members, friends and business associates.

Meanwhile, with the wireless not working, unsent messages had piled up high, constantly arriving through a pneumatic tube that connected the radio room with the purser's office. The result was a huge backlog of work that would have to be attended to once the transmitter was up and running again.

As soon as the set was fixed, Phillips began working non-stop, converting each message into Morse Code and tapping out their 'dits' and 'dahs' to the receiving station at Cape Race. As he did, *Titanic* continued to speed through the night directly toward the deadly ice that lay ahead – despite the many warnings she had received, including the latest from the *Mesaba* and *Amerika*, which never left the radio room.

The Fourth Circumstance
Signing off for Bed

As it sailed a few miles ahead of the *Titanic,* the 447-foot *Californian*, a Leyland Line freighter, almost found itself the victim of ice as well on the evening of 14 April. Despite the dark, moonless night, Captain Stanley Lord had spotted a large ice field lying directly in the path of his ship – and just in time. He turned the helm hard to starboard and reversed engines – but not before his ship had nudged into the edge of the ice. Although there was no damage to his ship, which carried only a cargo of lumber and no passengers, Lord was not taking any chances. He decided to stop for the night and proceed in the morning when daylight would aid him through the bergs and growlers spread wide before his ship.

Just before 11.00 pm, as he prepared to leave the bridge for the night, Lord spotted what he thought appeared to be the lights of another ship steaming up from the horizon. But he was not completely sure and thought it might be a rising star instead. Curious, Lord stuck his head into the wireless room where he found the ship's lone radio operator, Cyril Evans, sitting at his set. The captain asked if there were any other ships nearby and Evans replied, 'Only the *Titanic.*' Lord told Evans to call her up and let her know that they were stopped just ahead of her and surrounded by ice.

As instructed, Evans fired up his radio set and began messaging the *Titanic.* Using slang common among radio operators of the day, Evans casually tapped out the following on his telegraph key:

Say OM [old man] we are stopped and surrounded by ice.

13

But the close distance of the two ships made the *Californian*'s spark-generated signal very strong – and very loud – and it nearly blasted the headphones off Jack Phillips' ears as he sat at *Titanic*'s radio just a few miles back. Phillips – who was still busily working to clear the large backlog of passengers' telegrams – had been trying to copy a static-filled message from Cape Race when Evans' signal broke in and drowned it out. Angered by the intrusion, Phillips grabbed his telegraph key and pounded out a response:

Shut up, shut up! I am busy; I am working Cape Race!

With that harsh brush-off, Evans stopped transmitting and never sent any further information about the location of his ship or the vast expanse of ice that had forced her to stop. Phillips' rude rebuke of Evans' effort meant *Titanic* would never know of the danger floating in the ocean just a few miles ahead of her.

***

Evans listened to *Titanic*'s wireless messages a bit longer, but he was dead-tired and anxious for the next few minutes to pass so he could shut down his radio set as soon as his shift ended at 11.30 pm. When the hands of the clock finally indicated he was done for the day, Evans lost no time in turning off his wireless set and getting ready for bed. As the *Californian* had only one radio operator, there was no one to replace him. He cast his headphones aside and wearily climbed into his bunk for some much-welcome sleep. Across from where he lay, the clock in the radio room showed it was now 11.33 pm.

Just seven minutes later – at 11.40 pm – *Titanic* would hit the iceberg. Less than a half hour later, Jack Phillips would begin sending out frantic distress calls for help as the ice-cold water of the North Atlantic flooded into the ship's ruptured hull.

A few miles away, Evans was already fast asleep in his warm bunk.

***

Around midnight, as soon as Captain Smith had given the word, Jack Phillips had begun transmitting frantic calls for help over *Titanic*'s powerful 5,000-watt radio set. Phillips started by sending the distress call *CQD* – the long-standing international distress signal in use at that time. It stood for 'calling any station' (CQ) and 'distress' (D). But at the suggestion of Harold Bride, his fellow operator, Phillips would intersperse *CQD* with the new distress call that had recently been adopted – *SOS*.

'It may be the last chance you get the use it,' Bride said half-jokingly.

The logs of the rescue ship SS *Carpathia* support the recollection of Harold Bride, who served as *Titanic*'s second Radio Officer. According to both, when Captain Smith gave the order to radio for assistance, Phillips first sent '*CQD*' six times followed by the *Titanic* call letters, '*MGY*'. Later, at Bride's suggestion, Phillips also interspersed his calls with the newly adopted international distress signal '*SOS*.'

While many may think those letters stand for 'Save Our Souls' or 'Save Our Ship,' they actually stand for neither. '*SOS*' was simply chosen because it was easy to distinguish on the air, even through heavy static or when signals were weak. The Morse Code pattern of 'dit-dit-dit, dah-dah-dah, dit-dit-dit (... --- ...)' could easily be picked out of the ether by even the most novice telegrapher.

The 1918 Marconi Yearbook of Wireless Telegraphy and Telephony states: 'This signal [SOS] was adopted simply on account of its easy radiation and its unmistakable character. There is no special signification in the letter themselves, and it is entirely incorrect to put full stops (pauses) between them [the letters].'

Stations hearing this distress call were to immediately cease handling their regular radio traffic until the emergency was over. They were also required to answer the distress signal when it was received. But, although the use of '*SOS*' was officially ratified in 1908 – four years before the *Titanic* disaster – the use of '*CQD*' lingered for several more years, especially in the British service where it originated.

As radio technology was fairly primitive in the early 1900s, ships and coastal stations normally would go silent twice an hour to listen for distress signals. The silent period lasted three minutes and was observed at 15 and 45 minutes past each hour. However, many merchant vessels at that time only carried one radio operator, meaning a distress call might not be heard by an operator who was off-duty, as happened in the case of the *Californian* with its lone radio operator.

But because of incidents like the one involving the *Californian*, equipment was eventually invented to summon off-duty radio operators by ringing an alarm in their berths. The alarm was triggered when the radio operator of a ship in distress transmitted twelve long dashes of four seconds each. These signals were transmitted before sending *SOS* in the hope of ringing the automatic alarm aboard ships that had the system installed. Sometimes the *SOS* would also be delayed for a few moments to give radio operators who were 'off-watch' time to get to their radio rooms. Later, it was required that ships staff their radio rooms around the clock.

***

Prior to the end of his shift at midnight, the *Californian*'s Third Officer, Charles Groves, had been on deck making his usual rounds. It was around 11.10 pm when he also saw the lights of a big ship steaming up from the horizon. He could tell it was a large liner because he could make out its multiple, brightly-lit decks.

After a while, he went to Captain Lord's compartment to inform him of what he had seen. He estimated that the ship was no more than 8 to 10 miles away. Lord, who had also spotted the ship shortly before he had gone to his cabin, told Groves to try and contact her with the ship's Morse lamp. With that, Groves left to fulfil the captain's order and he spent several minutes signalling the other ship with Morse Code, using the shutters in front of the light to form the short 'dits' and longer 'dahs.' Despite repeated attempts, he received no response and eventually stopped signalling.

At midnight, Second Officer Herbert Stone took over the watch and Groves briefed him, including his attempt to signal the large liner he had spotted. Stone also tried the Morse lamp, but had no better luck in making contact.

Around 12.15 am, his shift over, Groves also headed down to his cabin to turn in for a while. But, as he often did, he decided to stop first by the wireless shack to see if he could pick up anything on the ship's radio set. He had become fascinated with this new technology and his visits were usually welcomed by Evans, who spent most of his time working alone in the radio room.

Groves had even become fairly good at picking out words from the streams of dits and dahs that made up the Morse Code. But with Evans fast asleep, he was not quite sure how the equipment operated and did not realise he needed to wind up the detector to make the set work. Meanwhile, *Titanic* continued making desperate pleas for help, but they would go unheard aboard the nearby Leyland liner.

Groves put on the headphones and spent a few moments unsuccessfully fiddling with the *Californian*'s radio. Hearing nothing, he took the headset off and placed it back on the table – and left.

***

Meanwhile, up on the bridge of the idled *Californian*, Stone saw a flash on the horizon around 12.45 am. At first, he thought it might have been a shooting star. But then there was another – and another. He called down the speaking tube to Captain Lord to tell him that he had seen rockets being fired.

Regulations at the time called for an emergency at sea to be signalled by firing five rockets at regular intervals of one minute each. But these rockets seemed to be going up at more irregular intervals. Stone and Lord discussed it briefly, but decided it was probably some sort of 'company' signals, so no action was taken. There was also no discussion about waking their sleeping radio operator to see if anything more could be learned.

Eventually, the lights of the nearby liner seemed to disappear, as though she was turning away from the *Californian*'s position. In reality, the *Titanic*'s lights *were* disappearing – under the water as she continued to sink by the bow. But the visual illusion it gave was that she was simply sailing away.

Shortly after 4.00 am, Chief Officer George Stewart relieved Stone and soon noticed another brightly-lit steamship was approaching from the south. It, too, was firing rockets into the air.

After a while, Stewart went to the radio room to wake Evans and ask him to find out what was going on. The groggy radio operator wiped the sleep from his eyes and fired up his wireless set. He quickly learned that the *Titanic* had sunk just 90 minutes or so before, at 2.20 am. The ship Stewart had seen was the *Carpathia*, rapidly steaming up from the horizon to rescue the 705 people who had survived the disaster.

***

The radio equipment on board the *Titanic* was the best available at the time, built and installed by the Marconi Company, far and away the biggest provider of radio equipment and radio operators at the time.

The transmitting system was powered by a 5-kilowatt motor-generator, which was backed up by both an emergency generator and batteries. The ship's radio had a guaranteed range of 250 miles under any weather conditions, and could usually communicate over 400 miles – and even farther if atmospheric conditions were particularly good, as they often were at night. The antenna system was made up of four wires strung 205 feet high between *Titanic*'s two masts – one of which was located just behind the bow and the other just forward of the stern.

The radio transmitter was known as a 'spark' type, operated with a standard telegraph key. The ship's radio system was primitive by today's standards and was actually set up in two separate rooms to minimise the 'buzzing' interference the transmitter would otherwise create with the receiver. Transmission signals were basically generated through brute force.

But although the *Californian* was well within range of the *Titanic*'s powerful radio set, the closest ship to actually *hear* her distress calls was the Cunard liner *Carpathia*, which was 58 miles away when it first picked up the pleas for assistance. But it was only by good luck that it heard those pleas.

Ironically, *Carpathia*'s radio operator, Harold Cottam, had also finished his shift and was off-duty when *Titanic* began sending its calls of *CQD* and *SOS*. Having spent some time on the bridge providing a briefing on the day's communications traffic, he had returned to the *Carpathia*'s radio room and was preparing to turn in for the night. While he was on the bridge, he had missed the *Titanic*'s first call for help.

Cottam had been on duty late the last two nights and had made up his mind to be in bed early this evening, but he found himself still up despite the fact it was now after midnight. As he undressed for bed, it was only by fortunate circumstance that he even heard *Titanic*'s frantic cries in the night. He had left his radio set on so he could listen to the news being sent from the shore station at Cape Cod to ships at sea.

After the news bulletins of the day concluded – and before shutting down his set for the night – Cottam happened to hear the Cape Cod station advising it had private traffic for the *Titanic*. Thinking it would be helpful to relay this information to White Star's newest liner, he turned on his transmitter and began to reach out to her. Within moments, *Titanic*'s radio operator, Jack Phillips, was back to him with a desperate plea for help:

Come at once. We have struck a berg. It's a CQD OM.

Interviewed by the BBC in 1956, Cottam vividly remembered what had happened that night so long ago. After receiving Phillips' message requesting assistance, Cottam initially found it hard to believe that such a magnificent new ship – especially one that had been labelled 'unsinkable' – could actually be in trouble.

'I said "Was it serious?" and he said "Yes it's a CQD OM [old man]. Here's the position, report it, and get here as soon as you can".'

Cottam took *Titanic*'s message and co-ordinates and rushed to the bridge to tell the senior officer on watch what was going on. But the crew members on the bridge were sceptical – likely because wireless was a new technology – and because the *Titanic* had the reputation of being the safest ship afloat. Surely, they thought, Cottam had got the message wrong.

'The information didn't seem as though it had sunk in as fast as I thought it ought to,' Cottam recalled. 'So I rushed down the ladder and knocked on the captain's cabin and – as I saw a light – I rushed in.'

'He said, "Who the hell?" – or words to that effect. So I said, "Well, the *Titanic* has struck ice, sir, and she's in distress. I've got the position here."

"Well, give it to me", he said and he put a dressing gown on and went.'

Cottam's account of what happened next appeared in *The New York Times* on 19 April 1912:

> We steamed with every ounce of speed in us in the direction given by the *Titanic*, and we reached the spot just before dawn. All this time we were hearing the *Titanic*, sending her wireless out over the sea in a last call for help. 'We are sinking fast', was one which I picked up being sent to the *Olympic*.

The last message Cottam received from Jack Phillips was:

> Come quick our engine room is flooded up to the boilers.

After that he did not hear anything more and began thinking this meant the great ship had sunk, as he told the chairman of the U.S. Senate hearing that was held a few days after the *Titanic*'s sinking:

Senator Alden Smith:
'I thought I understood the captain [Rostron of the *Carpathia*] to say that one of the last messages told the sinking ship that they [*Carpathia*] were within a certain distance and coming hard, or coming fast.'

Mr Cottam:
'I called him with that message, but I got no acknowledgement.'

Senator Smith:
'Just tell us what that message was. You called him with that message?'

Mr Cottam:
'Yes, sir.'

Senator Smith:
'We would like to know about that – just tell what it was.'

Mr Cottam:
'The captain told me to tell the *Titanic* that all our boats were ready and we were coming as hard as we could come, with a double watch on in the engine room, and to be prepared, when we got there, with lifeboats. I got no acknowledgement of that message.'

Senator Smith:
'But you sent it?'

Mr Cottam:
'Yes, sir.'

Senator Smith:
'Whether it was received or not, you don't know?'

Mr Cottam:
'No, sir.'

Senator Smith:
'Let us understand. When you received that last call from the *Titanic*, that her engine room was filling with water, you say you acknowledged its receipt and took that message to the captain. Did you acknowledge its receipt before you took it to the captain?'

Mr Cottam:
'Yes, sir.'

Senator Smith:
'Then, after you had taken this message to the captain, you came back to your instrument and sent the message that you have just described?'

Mr Cottam:
'Yes, sir.'

Senator Smith:
'And to that you received no reply?'

Mr Cottam:
'No, sir.'

Senator Smith:
'And you never received any other reply?'

Mr Cottam:
'No, sir.'

Senator Smith:
'Or any other word from the ship?'

Mr Cottam:
'No, sir.'

***

Although 58 miles does not seem like much of a distance, the *Carpathia* was an older ship and normally cruised at only 14.5 knots per hour – which translates to little more than 16.5 miles per hour. At that speed Rostron knew it would take well over three hours to reach the stricken *Titanic*. He quickly determined that the only way to coax some extra speed out of the old girl was to divert all of the steam her boilers could produce into the engines. He gave the order to the engine room and *Carpathia* begrudgingly responded, offering another 3.5 knots of speed.

Although most of the passengers on board Rostron's ship were asleep, some would soon wake up shivering because their staterooms had neither heat nor hot water. Others would be awakened by the clattering of activity on deck and the voices of the crew as they readied the ship to receive *Titanic*'s survivors. Lifeboats were swung out, coffee was made, blankets were stacked and medical supplies were prepared. Meanwhile, *Carpathia* sped to the rescue as fast as she could with Rostron dodging icebergs and growlers as quick as his lookouts could spot them.

But despite the heroic effort of the *Carpathia*, she would not reach the *Titanic*'s reported position until more than an hour after she sank. Once on the scene, all that would be found among the debris was the handful of lifeboats that held the 705 souls who had managed to get off the ship before she foundered. Rostron could hardly believe this had been where a great ship had surrendered to the sea. In his appearance before the Senate committee that investigated the disaster, he recalled the stark scene:

> I saw several empty boats, some floating planks, a few
> deck chairs, and cushions; but considering the size of the

disaster, there was very little wreckage. It seemed more like an old fishing boat had sunk.

***

The circumstances of Cottam's good fortune in accidentally hearing the *Titanic's* plea for help – and Captain Rostron's skilled handling of *Carpathia* through treacherous ice – would soon be widely credited with saving the wreck's survivors from the harsh elements of the frigid North Atlantic.

Both Rostron and Cottam received a 'hero's welcome' when they reached New York two days after the disaster. Rostron was awarded a Congressional Gold Medal by the U.S. Congress, and in 1926, he was appointed Knight Commander of the Order of the British Empire. He rose to become the Commodore of the entire Cunard fleet before retiring in 1931.

Meanwhile, Cottam continued to work at sea for another 10 years before finally giving up his ocean-going life to become a landlubber. He would even leave his career as a radio operator behind, getting married and taking a job as a sales representative.

As for the *Carpathia* herself, she would serve in the First World War transporting Allied troops and supplies. On 17 July 1918, she was part of a convoy travelling from Liverpool to Boston when she was struck by three torpedoes from a German U-boat and sank off the southern coast of Ireland. Five people were killed, but the rest of the passengers and crew were rescued by the HMS *Snowdrop*. In 1999, the wreck of the *Carpathia* was discovered intact and lying upright at a depth of some 500 feet below the surface.

In retrospect, Cottam's decision to stay up and spend a few minutes listening to the news on his ship's radio was one of the very few circumstances that broke in favour of the *Titanic* that night. At the Senate hearing, Captain Rostron recalled that catching her distress calls was only sheer luck:

The whole thing was absolutely providential. I will tell you this, that the wireless operator was in his cabin, at the time, not on official business at all, but just simply listening as he was undressing. He was unlacing his boots at the time. He had this apparatus on his ear, and the message came. That was the whole thing. In 10 minutes, maybe he would have been in bed, and we would not have heard the messages.

Sadly, there would be too many other unfavourable circumstances that would work overwhelmingly against *Titanic* this night.

The Fifth Circumstance
An Accomplice Moon, a Dead Calm Sea and a Missing Key

14 April 1912 brought with it a remarkable night. The sky was filled with stars, although the moon was but a dark disc and the sea was a dead, flat calm. In fact, it was the most well behaved some had ever seen the North Atlantic. The temperature had also rapidly dropped below freezing, leaving the two lookouts in *Titanic*'s crow's nest shivering to keep warm. Far below, the ship's engineers were busy amid fears that the tanks holding the ship's fresh water would freeze. As the ship drove through the icy sea, it not only lowered the temperature of the hull, but also the fresh water tanks nestled against it.

Although this bitter cold night was clear and starry, it was still difficult to see what lay ahead in the vast North Atlantic without the aid of moonlight. It was even harder to see without the aid of binoculars. The lookouts, Frederick Fleet and Reginald Lee, had asked about the 'glasses' but were told there were none to be had – even though they had a pair in the crow's nest during *Titanic*'s trip from Belfast to Southampton.

A last-minute change of *Titanic*'s crew literally held the key to their access. The original Second Officer, David Blair, had been removed from the ship's roster just before it left Southampton. In the rush, Blair had forgotten to give the officer who replaced him the key to the locker where the binoculars were stored. Without access to the glasses, the lookouts in the crow's nest were forced to rely solely on their eyes, watering from the cold as *Titanic* rushed through the darkness. By the time the lookout spotted the iceberg, there would only be 37 seconds until the impact. Even a few more seconds of warning might have averted the disaster, but it was not to be.

Later, at the U.S. Senate hearings held on the disaster, Fleet stated his belief that having binoculars could have made the difference:

> Senator Francis G. Newlands:
> 'Suppose you had had glasses such as you had on the *Oceanic*, or such as you had between Belfast and Southampton, could you have seen this black object (the iceberg) a greater distance?'
>
> Mr Fleet:
> 'We could have seen it a bit sooner.'
>
> Senator Newlands:
> 'How much sooner?'
>
> Mr Fleet:
> 'Well, enough to get out of the way.'
>
> Senator Newlands:
> 'Did you and your mates discuss with one another the fact that you had no glasses?'
>
> Mr Fleet:
> 'We discussed it all together, between us.'
>
> Senator Newlands:
> 'Were you disappointed that you had no glasses?'
>
> Mr Fleet:
> 'Yes, sir.'

Senator Newlands:
'I want to ask just one question. Can you see with glasses at night as well as during the day?'

Mr Fleet:
'Yes, sir.'

***

According to some researchers and weather experts, there may have been another circumstance that would help seal *Titanic*'s fate. Ten minutes before the collision with the iceberg, Fleet noticed a slight haze on the horizon ahead. He thought little of it, but some who have studied the possible atmospheric conditions of that night now believe what Fleet actually saw was a mirage created by the cold ocean waters meeting with the warmer air at the surface. The effect is similar to that seen in the desert when a mirage of water seems to appear. In this case, the effect would have created a visual anomaly that would have made the horizon actually seem higher. As a result, anything far away – such as an iceberg – could have been masked from view.

Fleet and Lee were at another disadvantage as well. The sea was a dead calm, with the ocean's surface as flat as a piece of plate glass. With no wind or swells to kick up the water, there would be no waves breaking against the base of any iceberg that might be out there – and therefore there would be no foaming white spray to signal a warning of what was ahead. This night there would be no such advantage – and without it – no extra time to steer a ship safely out of harm's way.

***

The night of 14 April had also brought with it a waning crescent moon. As a result, just a tiny sliver of its surface would reflect sunlight, providing only 5 per cent of a full moon's brightness. Any iceberg or growler lying ahead of *Titanic* would remain obscured in the darkness. This was emphasised by Second Officer Charles Lightoller when he testified about the circumstances leading up to the disaster during the British Inquiry into the sinking. He summed it up in a single sentence. 'In the first place, there was no moon,' he said. But, despite the fact *Titanic* was virtually blind that night, she would keep ploughing ahead – and at nearly her top speed.

***

The moon's near total absence that night may have only been part of its involvement in *Titanic*'s sinking. Four months earlier, it may have been responsible for the unusually large number of icebergs that came to be found in the North Atlantic shipping lanes by mid-April 1912.

On 4 January of that year, the Moon was the closest it had been to Earth in over a thousand years. This coincided with a rare confluence of other astronomical events that combined to simultaneously create both a spring tide and a perigean tide. Their combined forces resulted in much higher tidal ranges than normal.

A spring tide occurs when a new or full Moon lines up with the Sun to exert both of their combined gravitational pulls on the Earth and its oceans. Meanwhile, perigean tides take place when the Moon is closest to the Earth. The effect on the Earth becomes even greater if it is also at perihelion – when its orbit brings it closest to the Sun.

On 4 January, all of these astronomical events took place simultaneously, resulting in an estimated 74 per cent higher force on the planet's tides than when the Moon is at its mean distance from Earth. So how would this affect the *Titanic*'s sinking some four months later? Researchers who have looked at this rare event believe those higher tides may have done two things.

The first would have been to increase the 'calving' of glaciers in Greenland, allowing higher tides to help large chunks of them to break free, fall into the ocean and become menacing icebergs.

The second – and more probable cause as to why such a large number of bergs were in the North Atlantic – would have been the re-floating of massive bergs that had gone aground along the coastlines of Greenland, Labrador and Newfoundland, some of which may have been stranded for years. Once freed, ocean currents would have carried them south into the busy shipping lanes by April.

This phenomenon was first noted in the late 1970s by Fergus Wood, a tidal expert at the National Ocean Survey (now National Oceanic and Atmospheric Administration). Belgian astronomer Jean Mecus later did additional research to find that one would have to go back to the year 796 to find a closer lunar perigee, or forward to the year 2257 for the next.

To further support his theory, Wood wrote in the *Journal of Coastal Research* in 1995 that the extremities of the Jakobshavn Glacier would flex greatly in response to these higher-than-normal tides – especially given the astronomical circumstances of 4 January 1912. He concluded that the calving that produced the iceberg, which sank the *Titanic*, occurred on or around that date. However, critics of his theory believe it is unlikely that an iceberg would have been able to travel nearly 1,900 miles in just four months – the distance it would have to go from its supposed origination point to the spot where it met *Titanic*.

Instead, more credence is given to the idea that the spring and perigean tides of January 1912 – as well as nearly similar lunar events in December 1911 and February 1912 – combined to raise tidal levels that re-floated icebergs that had been stranded along the coasts of Newfoundland and Labrador. Upon renewing their voyages southward, they would have had time to reach the busy shipping lanes by the middle of April – and into *Titanic*'s path.

The Sixth Circumstance
The Deadly Battle of Vanity versus Design

The White Star Line never officially said that *Titanic* was 'unsinkable' – but it did nothing to dissuade the reputation that accompanied its new superliner. A spring 1911 issue of *Shipbuilder* magazine had carried a feature story which described the new *Olympic*-class liners as being 'practically unsinkable.' Soon it would become just 'unsinkable' in common use.

Still, White Star was not taking any chances. It took out a $5 million insurance policy on the hull of the ship, which was covered by such companies as the Atlantic Mutual Insurance Company of New York City. The first premium of $100,000 was paid before the *Titanic* set sail.

But although everyone was quite confident that *Titanic* represented the ultimate in seagoing safety, the ship was actually doomed before she ever left the drawing boards of Harland & Wolff.

When Thomas Andrews laid out the design of the *Olympic*-class liners for White Star, the worst accident he could image was a collision amidships, with the other possibility being a front-end collision that would damage the bow.

With that in mind, he designed a series of sixteen watertight compartments – any two of which could be flooded without the ship foundering. In a frontal collision, the first four compartments could be flooded and she would still float. It sounded like the perfect solution for the ultimate in safety at sea. Andrews was convinced that *Titanic* had actually been designed to be its own lifeboat.

31

But Andrews did not foresee the eventuality of his ships being turned so that an entire side would be exposed to an obstacle such as an iceberg, or that a finger of ice would breach hull plating below the waterline over the course of more than four compartments. His plans simply did not predict that five or six front compartments would be opened to the sea on a cold, frigid April night. But he would be aboard her maiden voyage and learn first-hand how badly he had miscalculated. And it would cost him his life.

Within minutes after *Titanic* struck the iceberg – the very one she had been warned about in advance – Andrews was below decks assessing her future. After a quick tour of the flooding compartments, he made a few computations. It quickly became clear to him that *Titanic* did not have much time left. Despite his best efforts to make her the safest ship afloat – despite changes to make her even better and safer than *Olympic* – Andrews knew it would not be long before his great creation would be lying on the seabed.

It was also very clear to him why his design had failed – the watertight bulkheads did not extend all the way up to the top deck. They were watertight horizontally, but not vertically.

It is not that Andrews did not want them built higher – he had simply been overruled early on by the President of the White Star Line, Bruce Ismay. Ismay had told Andrews to lower the bulkheads so that the *Titanic*'s decks could be made wider and more spacious, especially for its wealthy clientele in first class. Now, Andrews faced the fact that some of these critical partitions were only 10 feet above the waterline. Ismay's decision would prove to be fatal for more than 1,500 people – although not to Ismay himself. Before the ship's certain death, he would find his way into the safety of a lifeboat.

Much like an ice cube tray held at an angle under a tap, each compartment in the ruptured bow would fill up, one after another. As water reached the top of each shortened bulkhead, the loss of buoyancy would pull the bow further down and the inrushing sea would simply overflow into the next compartment behind it. The process would continue until *Titanic* could no longer survive, its ability to float gone.

Based on his inspection of the damaged ship, Andrews figured that seawater was flooding in at a rate of about 7 tons per second – fifteen times faster than *Titanic*'s pumps could dump it back overboard. As Andrews finished his calculations, he realised the shorter bulkheads that were supposed to improve the comfort of passengers would instead cost two-thirds of them their lives.

He put *Titanic*'s remaining life at two hours, perhaps a little more, depending on how long the pumps could continue to operate and delay the inevitable.

The Seventh Circumstance
A Combination of More Vanity and Outdated Regulations

Even with the flawed bulkhead design, there should still have been a way to save most – if not all – of the more than 2,200 souls on board *Titanic* that night. But again, the owners of the White Star Line had placed their desire for aesthetics over the need for safety.

Originally, *Titanic* had been designed to carry as many as sixty-four lifeboats and each davit on deck was capable of holding a total of three boats. This arrangement, along with other emergency boats and rafts to be placed on board, would have easily permitted a seat for everyone – even if the *Titanic* had left with the full complement of passengers and crew that she was designed to carry, a total of 3,547.

Although Thomas Andrews and *Titanic*'s chief technical designer, Alexander Carlisle, believed forty-eight lifeboats would be sufficient, Bruce Ismay and other White Star executives thought differently. When they saw a mock-up of her decks heavy with lifeboats, they decided it looked much too cluttered and might even cause members of the travelling public to doubt the ship's safety. Ismay proclaimed a lesser number would do – a much lesser number.

To set itself apart from its main competitor, Cunard, the White Star Line preferred to emphasise the amount of space available for the enjoyment of its passengers. Lifeboats blocked views and consumed valuable deck space and the company's directors, especially Bruce Ismay, would have none of this. As a result, *Titanic*'s lifeboats would be arranged on each side of the ship at the bow and stern – with

190 feet of open deck space between them. Certainly, it was no coincidence the area free of lifeboats was also along the first-class promenade.

Clearly, the issue was not about money. Adding the additional lifeboats Carlisle wanted would only cost $16,000 – an insignificant sum on a ship being built for $7,500,000. But Carlisle had grown old and was not well, and he finally dropped his push for more boats. But the dispute over the lifeboats was rumoured to be high among the reasons why he decided to retire from Harland & Wolff in the middle of the project.

In the end, *Titanic* would have just twenty lifeboats with a capacity for just 1,178 of the 2,224 on board for her maiden voyage. Only 705 passengers and crew would actually find their way into them at the end.

***

Six years after the *Titanic* disaster, *Practical Shipbuilding* magazine reflected on the decision to limit the number of lifeboats:

> The fact that *Titanic* carried boats for little more than half the people on board was not a deliberate oversight, but was in accordance with a deliberate policy that, when the subdivision of a vessel into watertight compartments exceeds what is considered necessary to ensure that she shall remain afloat after the worst conceivable accident, the need for lifeboats practically ceases to exist, and consequently a large number may be dispensed with.

Besides White Star's belief that *Titanic* would be practically unsinkable, the decision by the company to reduce the number of lifeboats was further bolstered by its confidence that the ship would never have to be evacuated all at once. In the view of White Star's management, the busy North Atlantic route would ensure that there would always be ships nearby to provide assistance. Lifeboats would only be needed to ferry passengers from a stricken ship to the rescue vessels until everyone was safely evacuated.

This theory would even seem to be validated when *Titanic* was about to be constructed. In January 1909, the White Star liner RMS *Republic* collided with the SS *Florida* in a thick fog off Nantucket. In this case, the transfer system worked to perfection, with all of the *Republic*'s passengers taken safely to other ships before she sank. Of the six people who died in the accident, all were killed during the collision itself, not because of the sinking. This further convinced White Star officials that lifeboats for everyone were clearly not needed.

Unfortunately, for those aboard *Titanic*, this theory would not hold true. She would sink in just over two hours – well before the first rescue ship arrived on the scene. Logic would dictate the only way to have saved all her passengers and crew would have been to have a seat for each one in a lifeboat.

But recently another question has been raised as to whether more lifeboats would have actually made a difference to the number of lives that were saved.

Captain Smith's order to prepare the boats and begin loading passengers was made a little after midnight, approximately 20 minutes after the collision. At that point, there were little more than two hours before the ship would sink at 2.20 am.

It took several minutes to inform the crew and begin the process of preparing the boats, getting passengers into their lifebelts and then up on deck. There had also been no lifeboat drill and most aboard – including the crew – had no idea as to which lifeboat they had been assigned. Given the confusion and lack of preparation, it is almost certain there were additional delays.

Using a replica lifeboat from the 1996 film *Titanic*, the film's director, James Cameron, ran a simulation to learn how long it would take to load a lifeboat and get it launched. The test revealed that the process took more than 20 minutes. This appears to be confirmed by the actual time the first lifeboat was launched from *Titanic* – 12.24 am. As it was, the ship had only minutes left when the eighteenth and final boat was launched at 2.05 am. Two collapsible lifeboats floated off without any passengers at 2.15 am as the ship began to slip beneath the sea.

Given these facts and the lack of preparedness that night, it probably would have been extremely difficult to successfully launch many more lifeboats in a timely manner – even if they had been available.

***

What is more disturbing is the fact *Titanic* had well *exceeded* the minimum number of boats required to meet the safety laws in place at the beginning of 1912. White Star had completely met the legal requirements to operate the ship, even though the lifeboats could hold only half of those on board that night – and *only one-third* if she had been filled to her full licensed capacity of over 3,500 passengers and crew.

But under the prevailing maritime regulations when *Titanic* was placed in service, the number of boats legally required was still based on gross tonnage, or the size of a ship – *not* the actual number of passengers aboard. These regulations had been put in place in 1894, when the ships being built were far smaller.

By 1912, *Titanic* would be *460 per cent larger* than the biggest ship that existed when the rules were first published. In the eighteen years that followed, ships had gained the ability to carry not hundreds, but thousands of passengers. Yet the lifeboat requirements had remained exactly the same – continuing to completely ignore the actual number of lives aboard. As a result, *Titanic* only needed to carry a total of sixteen lifeboats to be completely legal to operate.

With the twenty she had aboard, she exceeded the minimum number by a full 20 per cent.

Even though there was awareness that this 'safety' margin was badly outdated, it would be of little comfort to those left behind on the morning of 15 April at 2.20 am as *Titanic* slid beneath the waters of the North Atlantic measuring -2 degrees Celsius (28 degrees Fahrenheit).

The Eighth Circumstance
Flawed Construction Materials

Over the many years since the sinking, there has been much debate about *Titanic*'s design and the materials used to build her – some of it based on conjecture and circumstantial evidence, and some based on established facts.

Following *Titanic*'s discovery in 1985, subsequent dives to the wreck recovered pieces of the ship which were forensically examined. This included rivets used to hold the ship together, as well as pieces of the plating used to construct her hull.

In *What Really Sank the Titanic*, published in 2008, researchers Jennifer Hooper McCarthy and Tim Foecke detailed how these bits and pieces of the ship suffered extreme differences in quality and strength. In addition, the construction methods used to build the various sections of *Titanic*'s hull were different, also resulting in different levels of strength and durability.

In the case of the rivets, two different types were used to hold *Titanic*'s hull plates together and form a watertight seal. Wrought iron rivets were used for the bow and stern sections, while stronger steel rivets were installed only in the middle sections of the ship. There were a couple of reasons for this.

First, *Titanic*'s designers felt the greatest stresses on the ship would be in the middle, as it spanned the troughs between ocean waves. Thus, steel rivets would provide the added strength they felt was needed there. Second, these steel rivets were seated by powerful hydraulic machines, which provided both stronger and more consistently finished rivets.

Unfortunately, the smaller spaces contained in the bow and stern made it difficult to use the large hydraulic riveting machines, so the iron rivets placed there were driven by hand instead. And, because men – not machines – did the work, the more malleable and weaker wrought iron rivets had to be used. This also helped to ensure that workers in the yard remained happy, since the jobs held by the riveting crews, working by hand, were highly valued and highly paid as they expertly formed the rounded heads on each end of these fasteners.

Regardless of how they were installed, the rivets were heated to red-hot and then placed in holes stamped in the hull plates that had been aligned with each other. The rivets would then be hydraulically pressed or pounded by hand to form the rounded heads at each end. As the rivets cooled, they would shrink and pull the metal plates tightly together, producing a watertight seal. All of this was quite acceptable as a building practice at the time, but there was another problem – and that was with the wrought iron rivets themselves.

Harland & Wolff was not the only yard busy cranking out ships in the early 1900s. There was a large and growing demand for new vessels of all types and that also meant a large and growing demand for labour and materials at shipyards all over Britain and Europe. At that time, however, batches of rivets were being produced by hand and it required skilled workers who had learned the process by first serving as apprentices. With the increased demand for materials, manufacturers found themselves forced to press much less experienced workers into service, and, as a result, the materials they produced started to vary greatly in quality.

The weak link in the wrought iron rivet-making process centred on the 'puddlers' – workers who would stir the molten hot iron ore and then draw off the impurities it contained, known as slag. This was a critical skill and an inexperienced puddler could easily produce a batch of wrought iron that was woefully substandard.

In fact, tests performed on iron rivets recovered from *Titanic* revealed large variations in the amount of slag they contained –

ranging from 1.1 per cent to as much as 12.8 per cent – well over four times what should be expected. In some cases, bits of slag were even visible to the naked eye, making up as much as 40 per cent of a rivet's shaft and head. This would leave them susceptible to fracturing when they underwent stress – just the kind of stress that could take place when a ship travelling at high speed collided with a massive object like an iceberg. Meanwhile, the steel rivets used in the middle section of the ship showed only microscopic impurities and much more resistance to fracture and breaking.

***

Immediately after *Titanic's* sinking – and for many years after – the common belief was that the edge of the iceberg had sliced a nearly continuous 300-foot-long gash in her side, much like a tin opener. Unfortunately, the damaged starboard side of the ship cannot be visually inspected as it is buried in some 60 feet of silt, having been driven into the seabed when she hit the bottom at an estimated 30 or so miles an hour.

But researchers now know the 'tin opener' theory is not what actually happened, thanks to an acoustic examination of the ship's starboard hull that is buried in the bottom. In 1997, it was reported that sonar returns of the damaged bow indicated that six openings – each less than the width of a person's hand – appear to have punctured the hull over the course of her six forward compartments. These opened the forepeak, the three holds and boiler rooms five and six to the sea.

Considering the forensic evidence produced by the rivets and metal plates recovered from the wreck, it now appears that the shock produced by the collision simply popped and shattered a large number of the iron rivets along *Titanic's* starboard side, allowing the watertight seal between her hull plates to separate and pop open.

Researchers also believe these flawed rivets were further weakened by the freezing water the *Titanic* was sailing through the night of the disaster. The ocean's temperature had dropped to -2 degrees Celsius (28 degrees Fahrenheit), making the slag-filled wrought iron brittle and less malleable.

To confirm this theory, metal from rivets recovered from the wreck were cooled to the conditions found in the North Atlantic the night of the disaster and then impact-tested. They shattered and broke apart. Meanwhile, modern rivet metal subjected to the same test flexed but did not fail like those from the *Titanic*. In fact, it is now believed that the ship's wrought iron rivets were so substandard that they appear to have already been near their maximum stress limits when they were installed.

There was also another manufacturing process that likely contributed to the ship's hull being breached. When the rivet holes were placed in the hull plates, they were 'cold punched' using a steam-driven ram. This would create tiny fractures outward from the rivet hole. Shipbuilders were aware of this issue, but believed the fractures would be secured by a rivet's 'clamping' effect once it was driven into the opening. However, the residual stresses from the punching process would have been significant, exerting a driving force on the cracks. Upon impact of the plate at low temperatures, these cracks could have grown in a brittle manner and linked up, resulting in failure of the plate, especially if a weakened rivet popped out under stress, releasing the 'clamp.'

***

But were *Titanic*'s construction materials and methods really any different from other ships built at that time? A report entitled *Metallurgy of the RMS Titanic* by Tim Foecke of the National Institute of Standards and Technology concluded that while the rivets and hull plates were substandard by today's criteria, they were the norm for the time. Following Foecke's detailed analysis of *Titanic*'s metallurgy, he concluded:

- 'There is evidently a large variation in properties among the 2000 plates that made up the hull of *Titanic*. This conclusion is based on the very different microstructures and fracture behaviour observed in the two plate samples recovered to date. This is a normal result of the variability of feedstock and rolling conditions in turn-of-the-century ironworks.'
- 'Steps could have been taken to heat-treat the steel to improve its fracture properties, but this knowledge was simply not available in 1911.'
- 'Given the knowledge base available to engineers at the time of the ship's construction, it is the author's opinion that no apparent metallurgical mistakes were made in the construction of the RMS *Titanic*.'

***

Given the enormous size of the *Titanic*, one might think it would have taken a massive breach of her hull to result in her sinking. But estimates performed by several different researchers have all come to the same conclusion – the total area of the hull opened to the sea by the collision was little more than 12 square feet overall. Still, the water rushing through her shattered hull plates was more than enough to overwhelm her pumps and pull her under in little more than two hours – breaking her in half in the process.

The Ninth Circumstance
Speeding Towards Disaster

Titanic was 92 feet wide and 882 ½ feet long, and it was 175 feet from her keel to the top of her four funnels. Her gross tonnage was 46,328 and she displaced 52,310 tons of water. She required a depth of 34 feet 7 inches to operate without going aground.

Far below her passenger decks, twenty-four double-ended and five single-ended boilers could feed the two reciprocating engines with enough steam to produce 46,000 horsepower. In turn, they would drive a pair of three-blade wing propellers and one four-blade centre propeller. At cruising speed, *Titanic* could run at better than 21 knots, or about 24 miles an hour. It was a remarkable feat for the largest moving object ever built by man up to that time.

But her speed and design would also contribute to her undoing. During *Titanic's* sea trials, several tests were made of her handling characteristics. They began in Belfast Lough and then moved into the open waters of the Irish Sea. For half a day, *Titanic* was driven at different speeds and put through a number of turns and manoeuvres.

During her sea trials, it was shown that it took 37 seconds from the time her helm was put hard over for her to begin turning in response. Ironically, the iceberg that doomed her was estimated to be less than a quarter of a mile away when it was first spotted – and *Titanic* would cover that distance in just 37 seconds. The steam-powered machinery used to steer the ship was powerful, but it still took time as it laboured to turn the 78-foot-long rudder and its 101 tons of weight.

One of the most important tests was an emergency 'crash stop'. While travelling near her rated cruising speed of 21 knots, the engines were reversed from full ahead to full astern. It would take 3 minutes and 15 seconds for her to fully stop – and a distance of approximately 800 yards, or nearly half a mile. The British maritime inspector aboard for the sea trials found her capabilities acceptable and even praised her performance.

But, in the end, *Titanic* could neither turn nor stop in time to avoid hitting the iceberg that would sink her.

***

The question has often been asked why *Titanic* was allowed to continue travelling so fast when it was well known that dangerous ice lay ahead. Captain Smith had stated that they would have to slow down if things became at all '*the least bit doubtful*,' but still he took no action to reduce his ship's speed, despite the multiple warnings about the menacing ice that had been received.

Smith's true reason for maintaining such a high speed will never be known, as he was among those lost when the ship went down. But speculation has persisted since the disaster that Captain Smith and Bruce Ismay, the White Star's Managing Director, thought it would attract much favourable publicity if *Titanic* arrived before its scheduled landing on Wednesday morning, 17 April at White Star's Pier 59 in New York.

However, there is conflicting evidence on this point – including written proof that Ismay appeared to be against early arrivals. In a letter dated 27 July 1911 to P. A. S. Franklin, the manager of the White Star office in New York City, Ismay wrote:

> Your strong recommendation that the Olympic, on her next voyage, should be allowed to dock on Tuesday evening, will receive consideration, and I note you say that she could have done this easily on her last voyage. I do not quite gather whether your recommendation goes so far as

to advocate our always attempting to land passengers on Tuesday; perhaps you will let me hear from you on this.

I at once admit that docking on Tuesday evening would help you in turning the ship round, and give those on board a better chance of getting the ship in good shape for the Saturday sailing, and further, that if we could make it a practice to do this, it would please the passengers, but as I have repeatedly stated, I feel very strongly that passengers would be far more satisfied to know, when they left here, that they would not land until Wednesday morning, rather than be in a state of uncertainty in regard to this for the whole of the trip. I do not think you can have ever experienced the miseries of a night landing in New York; had you done so, I think your views might be altered.

Ismay had also stated during his trip on *Titanic*'s maiden voyage that Captain Smith was in command of the ship and that he was just a passenger. Captain Rostron of the rescue ship *Carpathia* provided support to Ismay's testimony when he appeared before the U.S. Senate investigation:

Senator Smith:
'In your company, who is the master of a ship at sea?'

Mr Rostron:
'The captain.'

Senator Smith:
'In absolute control?'

Mr Rostron:
'In absolute control, legal and otherwise. No one can interfere.'

Later in his testimony, Rostron reiterated this position.

Senator Smith:
'Captain, is it customary to take orders from a director or a general officer of the company aboard?'

Mr Rostron:
'No, sir.'

Senator Smith:
'From whom do you take orders?'

Mr Rostron:
'From no one.'

Senator Smith:
'Aboard ship?'

Mr Rostron:
'At sea, immediately I leave port until I arrive at port, the captain is in absolute control and takes orders from no one. I have never known it in our company or any other big company when a director or a managing owner would issue orders on that ship. It matters not who comes on board that ship they are either passengers or crew. There is no official status and no authority whatever with them.'

So, if there is no direct evidence that Captain Smith was urged by anyone to continue driving the ship at full speed, then why does the question persist?

A more likely explanation for *Titanic*'s speed is that it was standard practice for liners to continue at their normal cruising speed, slowing down or taking evasive action only if they actually were confronted by dangerous conditions. This practice held even after dark.

Titanic had already been steered further south than normal and Smith likely believed there was minimal chance of encountering ice. He also would have had great faith in the ability of the ship's lookouts to spot ice in plenty of time to avoid it. In short, he was confident *Titanic*'s speed was not an issue to worry about. In addition, some believe Smith would have been reluctant to slow down the maiden voyage because he was also aware that his ultimate boss was aboard: Bruce Ismay, Chairman of the White Star Line.

At the British Inquiry which followed, Rostron again stated his regard for Smith and indicated that Smith's navigation of the ship was standard practice for the times:

> Attorney-General Sir Rufus Isaacs:
> 'Supposing you had had a report of the character that I have indicated to you of icebergs and an ice field in the regions which you are bound to cross, when you approach that region, would you take any precautions with regard to the safety of your vessel?'

> Mr Rostron:
> 'Well, a great deal would depend on the weather and the atmospheric conditions.'

> Commissioner Lord Mersey:
> 'Suppose it is perfectly clear?'

> Mr Rostron:
> 'If it is a perfectly clear night, and I was sure of my position and everything else, unless I knew there was a lot of ice about, I should feel perfectly justified in going full speed.'

> The Attorney-General:
> 'But if you thought there was a lot of ice about, you would not do it, I gather?'

> Mr Rostron:
> 'No, I would not. For one or two bergs I should feel perfectly justified in going full speed.'

The Commissioner:
'I suppose it is a matter for the judgement of the man in charge of the ship?'

Mr Rostron:
'Absolutely.'

The Attorney-General:
'Which again, I suppose, must depend upon the atmospheric conditions as to whether he can see clearly ahead?'

Mr Rostron:
'Yes. We have to take a whole lot of things into consideration in a thing of that kind. It is not one or two; it is many.'

Sir Robert Finlay (representing the White Star Line):
'Did you know Captain Smith?'

Mr Rostron:
'Yes.'

Sir Finlay:
'He was a very experienced Officer, I think?'

Mr Rostron:
'Yes, very.'

Sir Findlay:
'Of very high standing?'

Mr Rostron:
'Very high, indeed.'

But in the end, the British Enquiry into the disaster led by Lord Mersey would pin the cause of the disaster primarily on just one thing – *Titanic*'s excessive speed. It would infer that blame was placed squarely on Captain Smith, who had perished in the disaster and conveniently could not defend himself against the court's finding.

The *Report of a Formal Investigation into the circumstances attending the foundering on the 15th April, 1912, of the British Steamship Titanic* would sum it all up in just one sentence:

> The Court, having carefully enquired into the circumstances of the above mentioned shipping casualty, finds, for the reasons appearing in the Annex hereto, that the loss of the said ship was due to collision with an iceberg, brought about by the excessive speed at which the ship was being navigated.
>
> Dated this 30th day of July, 1912
> MERSEY, Wreck Commissioner

The Tenth Circumstance
A Slow Turning Ship and Only Seconds to Decide

There has also been much speculation as to whether *Titanic*'s rudder was large enough to turn such a massive ship quickly enough in the face of danger. In fact, by construction standards in place at the time, her rudder was *slightly* too small, but it was not considered enough of a factor to compromise her overall safety. However, as we have already learned, it would take well over 30 seconds for her to begin turning after the helm was put all the way over.

Evidence also exists that a larger rudder was not used because it would have required bigger and more expansive equipment to control it – and a significant redesign of the ship's aft steering compartment.

As it turned out, the greater problem with *Titanic*'s steering design was her centre propeller. Positioned directly in front of the rudder, the centre screw could be stopped – but not reversed. The thrust it produced while underway would increase the slipstream of water moving past the rudder and enhance its manoeuvring of the ship. But the rudder's ability to turn the great ship would be adversely affected if the centre propeller was stopped because its four blades would now drag against the water, blocking the smooth slipstream that the rudder acted upon to turn the ship.

Once the iceberg was spotted, First Officer William Murdoch, the man in charge of *Titanic*'s bridge at that time, went with his first instinct: avoid the looming iceberg by steering the speeding ship to port (left) and reversing the engines. His decision would seem the most logical, especially given the few seconds in which he had to make it. In truth, it meant *Titanic's* destruction.

First, reversing the engines – and the propellers they drove – would take precious time. The bridge did not directly control the engines, so it was necessary to relay orders to the engine room via the telegraph on the bridge. Then the engineers far below would have to open and close various valves that diverted the steam from the boilers that ran the engines.

As *Titanic's* two massive wing propellers ground to a halt and then reversed, they would now disrupt the smooth flow of water slipping past the rudder, making it much less effective in its ability to turn the ship. The problem would be further magnified by the blocking action of the now stagnant centre propeller, which could only be driven forward.

With the ship slowing, the laws of hydrodynamics would also kick in, greatly decreasing her rate of turn. In addition, the effect of the two outside propellers spinning in reverse would kick up cavitation around the propellers – a bubbling of the water which would produce air pockets and voids – further disturbing the smooth flow of water past the rudder.

As a result, *Titanic's* eventual swing to port was agonisingly slow and meant she would not clear the ice ahead, but rather expose her starboard side, allowing it to scrape along the icy tentacles extending outward from the berg under the water. In the end, these icy fingers would bump along the side of the ship, rupturing rivets and steel plates to open her forward compartments to the frigid water of the North Atlantic – and sealing her fate.

***

In retrospect, it seems it might have made much more sense to have reversed the engines and to have continued to steer directly into the berg and hit it head-on. This logic had even been outlined in 1910 in the publication *Knight's Modern Seamanship*:

> The first impulse of many officers in such a situation is to turn away from danger, and at the same time to reverse the engines with full power. This course is much more likely to cause collisions than prevent them. It may be right for 'the ship' to turn away, if the emergency is such as to call for any actions on her part; but if she does this, so far from reversing the engines, she should, if possible, increase her speed as her whole effort must be directed to getting 'out of the way of the obstacle' as quickly as possible... To turn away and slow is the surest possible way of bringing about collision.

This theory was further supported at the British Inquiry by the testimony of Edward Wilding, the Harland & Wolff naval architect who had worked on *Titanic*:

> Mr Sidney Rowlatt (Commission attorney):
> 'Perhaps I ought to put this general question to you. The contact with this iceberg was the contact of a body weighing 50,000 tons moving at the rate of 22 knots an hour?'
>
> Edward Wilding:
> 'Yes.'
>
> Mr Rowlatt:
> 'I gather to resist such a contact as that you could not build any plates strong enough, as plates?'
>
> Edward Wilding:
> 'It depends, of course, on the severity of the contact. This contact seems to have been a particularly light one.'

Mr Rowlatt:
'Light?'

Edward Wilding:
'Yes, light, because we have heard the evidence that lots of people scarcely felt it.'

Mr Rowlatt:
'You mean it did not strike a fair blow?'

Edward Wilding:
'If she struck it a fair blow I think we should have heard a great deal more about the severity of it, and probably the ship would have come into harbour if she had struck it a fair blow, instead of going to the bottom.'

Mr Rowlatt:
'You think that?'

Edward Wilding:
'I am quite sure of it.'

Lord Mersey (The Commissioner):
'I am rather interested about that. Do you mean to say that if this ship had driven on to the iceberg stem she would have been saved?'

Edward Wilding:
'I am quite sure she would, My Lord. I am afraid she would have killed every fireman down in the firemen's quarters, but I feel sure the ship would have come in.'

Lord Mersey:
'And the passengers would not have been lost?'

Edward Wilding:
'The passengers would have come in.'

Lord Mersey:
'Then do you think it was an error of judgement – I do not by any means say it was a negligent act at all – to starboard the helm?'

Edward Wilding:
'It is very difficult to pass judgement on what would go through an Officer's mind, My Lord.'

Lord Mersey:
'An error of judgement and negligence are two different things altogether. A man may make a mistake and be very far from being negligent?'

Edward Wilding:
'Yes.'

Lord Mersey:
'Do you think that if the helm had not been starboarded there would have been a chance of the ship being saved?'

Edward Wilding:
'I believe the ship would have been saved, and I am strengthened in that belief by the case which your Lordship will remember where one large North Atlantic steamer, some 34 years ago, did go stem on into an iceberg and did come into port, and she was going fast?'

Lord Mersey:
'I am old enough to remember that case, but I am afraid my memory is not good enough.'

Mr Frederick Laing (White Star counsel):
'The *Arizona* – I remember it.'

Edward Wilding:
'The *Arizona*, my Lord.'

Mr Rowlatt:
'You said it would have killed all the firemen?'

Edward Wilding:
'I am afraid she would have crumpled up in stopping herself. The momentum of the ship would have crushed in the bows for 80 or perhaps 100 feet.'

Mr Rowlatt:
'You mean the firemen in their quarters?'

Edward Wilding:
'Yes, down below. We know two watches were down there.'

Mr Rowlatt:
'Do you mean at the boilers?'

Edward Wilding:
'Oh, no, they would scarcely have felt the shock.'

Lord Mersey:
'Any person, fireman or anybody else, who happened to be in that 100 feet, would probably never have been seen again?'

Mr Rowlatt:
'The third-class passengers are there too, I think, some of them?'

Edward Wilding:
'I do not think there are any third-class passengers forward of the second bulkhead, and I believe she would have stopped before the second bulkhead was damaged. It is entirely crew there, and almost entirely firemen – firemen, trimmers, and greasers.'

Mr Rowlatt:

'Your opinion is that the ship would have suffered that crushing in the first two compartments, but that the shock would not have shattered or loosened the rivets in any other part of the ship?'

Edward Wilding:

'Not sufficiently. As it would take a considerable length, 80 or 100 feet to bring up, it is not a shock, it is a pressure that lasts three or four seconds, five seconds perhaps, and whilst it is a big pressure it is not in the nature of a sharp blow.'

Lord Mersey:

'It would, I suppose, have shot everybody in the ship out of their berths?'

Edward Wilding:

'I very much doubt it, My Lord.'

Lord Mersey:

'At 22 1/2 knots an hour, and being pulled up quite suddenly?'

Edward Wilding:

'Not quite suddenly, My Lord. 100 feet will pull up a motor car going 22 miles an hour without shooting you out of the front.'

Mr Rowlatt:

'What you mean is that the ship would have telescoped herself?'

Edward Wilding:

'Yes, up against the iceberg.'

Mr Rowlatt:
'And stopped when she telescoped enough?'

Edward Wilding:
'Yes, that is what happened in the *Arizona*.'

But to continue straight into an oncoming iceberg was to go against every sailor's instinct and training. Trying to swing to port and out of its path would clearly seem the more logical choice. Reversing the engines would make the turn less effective, but trying to analyse the effects of that decision in a matter of seconds was also probably not realistic. With the need for critical decisions to be made in just seconds, there was literally no turning back from them once they were made – right or wrong.

***

But would the *Titanic* have been better off if it had been driven straight into the iceberg?

As Edward Wilding believed, the ship's forward compartments would have absorbed the collision and no more than four compartments would have been breached, allowing the ship to remain afloat. Indeed, Andrews had envisioned the possibility of *Titanic* colliding head-on with another ship. But the dynamics of running into a massive and stationary object like an iceberg are much different.

With the collision of two ships, both share absorption of the impact with the water around them also dissipating some of the force. As Wilding stated in his testimony, *Titanic*'s forward bulkheads would have served as 'crumple zones' – much like those found on today's modern cars – meaning that they would absorb most of the energy of the impact following a collision. In a collision with another ship, both the vessels would probably suffer heavy damage, but the impact would be spread between them and they would likely survive, at least for a while.

For example, when the *Stockholm* collided broadside with the *Andrea Doria* in 1956, the latter ship remained afloat for several hours and didn't sink until the next day, providing time to rescue its crew and passengers. Meanwhile, the *Stockholm*, despite her badly crumpled bow, remained afloat and was able to return to New York under its own power. This is much the same scenario that Andrews had designed his *Olympic*-class ships to survive.

But had the *Titanic* slammed directly into the iceberg, it likely would have been a very different story.

First, the *Titanic* was over 46,000 tons and travelling at approximately 23 miles an hour or so. It is estimated this translated into a kinetic energy force of nearly 2,847,217,691 joules (2,100,000,000 foot-pounds). Meanwhile, the iceberg was stationary and massive, reaching an estimated height of as much as 100 feet and a length of 200 to 400 feet. With most of its mass under water, it has been estimated it weighed some 75,000,000 tons.

Given these facts, *Titanic* would have come to a very sudden and violent stop, not only crushing the front of the ship but also sending the force of the collision along its entire hull. This would have undoubtedly caused massive damage throughout the ship – especially given the weaker, hand-driven rivets holding her forward hull together.

While the bow would have certainly crumpled, the crushing forces placed on her from bow to stern would have also likely buckled seams all along her length, perhaps causing her to sink even faster than she did. As discussed in a later chapter, *Titanic* was also built using thinner and lighter steel than the original design called for in her hull plates. Their ability to withstand such violent forces is questionable as well.

In addition, passengers and crew – many of whom were asleep – would have almost certainly been severely injured as they were thrown about, perhaps making the death toll even larger than it was. No one is reported to have been badly injured or killed in the initial collision in which the ship's side scraped along the iceberg.

Of course, the scenario given here is based in large part on 'what ifs'. Unfortunately, all of the exact circumstances and necessary information to develop definitive answers to these questions disappeared with *Titanic* long ago.

But given the known physics, running headlong into the iceberg at high speed very likely would not have resulted in any better outcome for *Titanic* – or her passengers.

The Eleventh Circumstance
An Unsinkable Myth

In the early hours of 14 April, even as the bow of the *Titanic* slipped beneath the sea, second-class passenger Sylvia Caldwell asked a deckhand: 'Is this ship really unsinkable?' 'Lady, God himself could not sink this ship,' was his reassuring reply.

The myth that *Titanic* could not be sunk lasted almost until her very end, and it would cost many of those aboard their lives. The lacking sense of danger and fear was further perpetuated by the collision itself. Most passengers and crew hardly felt it and many did not think much of it at all.

Late on a Sunday night – and snug in their warm staterooms – many slept right through the impact with the berg. Others found little to be alarmed about, although some noticed a faint rumble followed by the absence of the distant hum of the ship's engines as they were stopped. One passenger later recalled that it felt little more than if the ship had rumbled over a thousand marbles.

'There's talk of an iceberg, ma'am, and they've stopped so as not to run over it,' Cabin Steward Walter Bishop told Mrs Arthur Ryerson, a passenger in first class. Bishop himself would not survive the night.

Another steward had a similar response for George Harder, who was also travelling in first class. 'Oh, it will be a few hours and then we'll be on our way again,' he calmly remarked.

Many of the crew even thought the collision to be more of an inconvenience than a danger. One thought the vibration he felt was due to a lost propeller blade. 'Another Belfast trip!' he remarked, thinking they would simply have to limp back to the Harland & Wolff shipyard for repairs.

Still, some were more curious and set out to see if they could learn more as to why the great liner had stopped. Few found anything to be concerned about. When passenger William T. Stead inquired as to what the problem was, he was told there were icebergs about. 'Well,' he replied, 'I guess it's nothing serious. I'm going back to read.'

Throughout the ship, the complacency lingered on. Even Captain Smith thought, at least in the first few minutes after the collision, that *Titanic* would survive. In his first visit to the radio room, he told Second Operator Harold Bride to try and get through to Cape Race and have them send a cable to the White Star Line that the ship was damaged but would proceed to Halifax. He said White Star should also be advised that repairs might be necessary at Harland & Wolff's Belfast yard.

It was only when Smith returned to the bridge that he learned the truth from *Titanic*'s designer, Thomas Andrews. He pulled the captain aside to tell him that it was a 'mathematical certainty' that the ship would sink.

Meanwhile, few, if any, of the passengers, had any idea that there was only enough room in the lifeboats for just over half of those on board. Even many of the crew members were unaware of the unbalanced arithmetic. But early on, it did not seem to matter. *Titanic* still seemed invincible, as well as warm, comfortable and inviting.

Twenty minutes after hitting the berg, second-class passenger Edwina Troutt was curious as to what was going on. She found a steward and asked him if he knew anything. As he continued to polish a brass fixture, he said nonchalantly, 'Oh, I've been in skirmishes before.' In his best cockney accent, he continued, 'I'm going to get me work done.'

Another couple had ventured from their stateroom to see a mail clerk whose trousers had become soaked as he retrieved letters from the rapidly flooding mail room. A passing steward quickly reassured them. 'Everything is alright now... you may turn in,' he told them. For most aboard the ill-fated ship, the myth of 'unsinkability' had been perpetrated for so long that it seemed impossible to think otherwise.

***

As far back as 31 May 1911, when the *Titanic* slid down the slipway and into the water for the first time, the White Star Line used the occasion of her launch to feed the newspapers details about how spectacular and safe its new ships were. The company's wordsmiths left little to the imagination in their carefully crafted press release:

> ...the White Star Line's new triple-screw steamers *Olympic* and *Titanic* epitomise all the science and skill of a century of steam navigation. The same spirit which actuated the White Star Line in introducing into the Atlantic passenger trade the steamers *Oceanic*, the first steamer to surpass the length of the *Great Eastern* – *Celtic*, *Cedric*, *Baltic*, and, latterly, the giant *Adriatic* – has produced these new surpassing ships.
>
> Figures speak most concisely and eloquently of the supremacy of the *Olympic* and *Titanic*. The largest plates employed in the hull are 36ft long, weighing four and a half tons each, and the largest steel beam used is 92ft long, the weight of this double beam being four tons.
>
> Further, the colossal rudder, which is to be operated electrically, weighs 100 tons, the anchors 15½ tons each, the centre turbine propeller 22 tons and each of the two wing propellers 38 tons.
>
> The huge after 'bossarms', from which are suspended the three propeller shafts, tip the scales at 73½ tons, and the forward 'bossarms' at 45 tons. It is also interesting to note that each link in the anchor chains weighs 175lb.

In each ship the unusually large number of sidelights and windows – over 2,000 – add much to the brightness and cheerful effect of the public rooms and passenger cabins.

As already intimated, nothing has been left to chance in the construction of these superb ships, and besides being the largest and heaviest vessels ever built, they are also undoubtedly the strongest.

Their towering hulls are molded to battle against the seven seas, and boast, in each ship, the presence of three million rivets (weighing about 1,200 tons) holding together the solid plates of steel. To ensure stability in binding the heavy plates in the double bottom of each ship a half million rivets, weighing about 270 tons, have been used.

While this information alone would seem to make these ships appear indestructible, the White Star Line continued on with its embellishments, providing further belief to the myth that they could survive any hazard.

Safety Assured

The double bottom referred to extends the full length of each vessel, varying from 5ft 3in. to 6ft 3in. in depth and lends added strength to the hull. The subdivision of the hulls of the *Olympic* and *Titanic* into fifteen compartments separated by watertight bulkheads of steel further assures the safety of the vessels.

The gigantic size of these steamers is best appreciated when it is recalled that in length each vessel overtops by 182½ ft the height of the Metropolitan Tower in New York – the highest office building in the world, and 132½ ft beyond the height of the new Woolworth building now under construction.

Each ship being four times as long as the height of the famous Bunker Hill Monument and 327ft longer than the height of the Washington Monument, their massive measurements far excel America's most famous memorials.

Bilge or fin keels prevent these fine steamers from rolling, and their machinery is the unique combination of reciprocating engines (operating the two wing propellers) and a low-pressure turbine (operating the centre propeller), an ideal arrangement which has been tested thoroughly and found most satisfactory from an engineering point of view in the White Star Line's Canadian service steamer *Laurentic*.

Spaciousness and Beauty

A rapid survey of the 11 steel decks of the *Olympic* and *Titanic* reveals the most careful and comprehensive preparations in every department. Three elevators in the First Class and one in the Second Class provide a comfortable means of access between decks, which, on ships so vast as these, saves the passenger much effort.

***

Despite these lofty accolades of comfort and safety, Captain Smith, his officers and Thomas Andrews quickly knew better – as did those far below in the forward boiler rooms which were now rapidly flooding.

And so, a conscious decision was made to avoid panic at all costs. The word to prepare to evacuate the ship was passed without fanfare, and the order went out calmly: load the lifeboats with women and children first, and then lower away. But even as the crew made the lifeboats ready, the complacency continued.

Although the ship's bow angled down and listed to starboard fairly rapidly within the first hour after the collision, the rate of her sinking appeared to slow during the second hour, adding only one additional degree of downward angle to the original four-degree dip. This led some aboard to believe the situation had come under control and there was a sense of hope that *Titanic* would stay afloat, at least until help arrived. In reality she was still flooding rapidly. The difference was the incoming water was now flowing more symmetrically as opposed to when her starboard side filled first with sea water, originally causing a lopsided list.

Besides complacency, there was another major problem. The crew and passengers alike had little understanding of how to react to the emergency. In fact, there had not been a single lifeboat drill during the voyage.

A drill had been scheduled the very day of the collision, but it had been cancelled by Captain Smith for some inexplicable reason that will never be known. The only lifeboat drill had been held back in Southampton prior to departure when a handful of the crew lowered the two forward boats and rowed around next to the ship for a while before being hoisted back aboard.

As a result of this lack of preparedness, most passengers had no idea to which boat they had been assigned in the event of an emergency. And with the biting cold, there were very few willing to step outside and into the little open boats they were now being urged to fill.

In fact, even the crew had little understanding of what to do. Of the 892 crew members aboard, only six were officers and only thirty-nine were able-bodied seamen. The rest of the ranks were made up of everything from waiters, cooks and stewards to the firemen, far below decks, who fed the boilers with coal. In addition, many of the crew had only joined *Titanic* just before she sailed. This left them with little time to learn about the great ship's layout, much less its emergency operations. Most had no idea to which lifeboat they themselves had been assigned, let alone to which ones the passengers should report. It is likely many, if not most, had never rowed a boat before.

***

Even Second Officer Charles Lightoller – a man with extensive experience at sea – found that when he first boarded the superliner, it had taken him two weeks to finally figure out how to get around *Titanic*'s labyrinth of decks and passageways without getting lost.

Now, Lightoller was suddenly responsible for helping to evacuate the sinking liner and he found the situation frustrating as he prepared to load lifeboat 6. There was no one waiting on deck to get in and there was little enthusiasm as he called for women and children to come forward. Some even refused outright.

'We are safer here than in that little boat,' said millionaire John Jacob Astor as he was offered a seat in a boat that was far from full. He would not survive his decision to remain on the sinking ship.

The same slow pace was taking place on the other side of *Titanic* as well. At lifeboat 7, a handful of passengers reluctantly came forward. A few ladies boarded first, but when no more single women would agree to get in, some couples were allowed, followed by a few single men. A smattering more arrived, but the lifeboat – which held 65 – was less than half full when, at 12.40 am, it became the first to be lowered into the freezing waters of the North Atlantic. It was slightly more than an hour since *Titanic* had struck the iceberg.

The boats were lowered in sequence, from the middle, forward toward the bow, then aft. First Officer William Murdoch, Third Officer Herbert Pitman and Fifth Officer Harold Lowe worked on the starboard side boats. On the port side, Captain Smith worked with Chief Officer Henry Tingle Wilde and Second Officer Charles Lightoller. *Titanic* also carried four collapsible lifeboats, but they would be handled last, as they could not be launched until the forward davits were clear.

Although Smith had ordered his officers to put the 'women and children in and lower away,' his command was taken with different meanings by Officers Murdoch and Lightoller. Murdoch thought the order meant that women and children were to be loaded *first*, and then, if there was still room in the boats, men could be allowed in.

Lightoller thought the order meant women and children *only* – and this resulted in Lightoller lowering lifeboats on the port side with empty seats if there were no women and children left to board. Meanwhile, on the starboard side, Murdoch would allow men to board – but only if all the nearby women and children had got in first. In the end, the chance of a man surviving greatly depended on which side of the ship he happened to seek space in a lifeboat.

***

In all, *Titanic* carried fourteen main lifeboats (designated 3 to 16), each 30 feet long and capable of carrying sixty-five people. Eight were located at the stern, with four on each side. Six more were located towards the bow in the same configuration. In addition, there was a pair of 25-foot-long wooden cutters that could hold forty people each, designated as boats 1 and 2. These were located furthest toward the bow and were swung out while the ship was underway for immediate use in case of an emergency, such as rescuing a person who had fallen overboard. Finally, there were the four collapsible rafts with canvas sides that could be pulled up to form a boat. These were designated A to D and they could carry forty-seven people each.

The launching of *Titanic*'s lifeboats gives further support to the premise that many of her passengers believed the ship was unsinkable. One only has to look at how few got into the first lifeboats as they were launched. It wasn't until approximately 1.30 am – as it became more apparent that the ship might not survive – that some lifeboats would finally leave with a full capacity.

Time	Lifeboat	Location	Capacity	Total Aboard
12.40 am	7	Starboard	65	28
12.43 am	5	Starboard	65	36
01.00 am	3	Starboard	65	32
01.00 am	8	Port	65	28

Time	Lifeboat	Location	Capacity	Total Aboard
01.05 am	1	Starboard	40	12
01.10 am	6	Port	65	28
01.20 am	16	Port	65	40
01.25 am	14	Port	65	58
01.30 am	12	Port	65	30
01.30 am	9	Starboard	65	56
01.35 am	11	Starboard	65	70
01.40 am	13	Starboard	65	65
01.41 am	15	Starboard	65	65
01.45 am	2	Port	40	17
01.50 am	10	Port	65	35
01.50 am	4	Port	65	42
02.00 am	Collapsible C	Starboard	47	44
02.05 am	Collapsible D	Port	47	25
02.15 am	Collapsible B	Port*	47	30
02.15 am	Collapsible A	Starboard*	47	12

* washed off the ship as it sank

There are also some other possible circumstances that added to the death toll. During the U.S. Senate inquiry into the disaster, testimony was heard from the ship's officers that they believed the lifeboats were at risk of buckling and breaking apart if they were lowered while fully loaded. They intended that once the boats reached the water, they would take passengers from doors in the ship's side or pick up passengers who had jumped in the water. But the first never happened – and the second circumstance only occurred after stranded passengers saw no alternative but to leap into the frigid water as *Titanic* sank.

In fact, the lifeboats had their keels reinforced with steel beams so they would not buckle under a full load while in the davits. Moreover, Harland & Wolff's Edward Wilding testified during the official hearings that the lifeboats had, in fact, been tested safely with the equivalent of a full load of passengers. However, that information was never passed on to the crew of *Titanic*. This lack of vital information likely contributed to the fact that many lifeboats were lowered away with much room to spare.

In all, the ship's lifeboats, including the four collapsible boats, would have held 1,178 passengers. But the rapid sinking of the ship made it impossible to properly launch all the boats, leaving the total capacity of those launched at only 1,084. Still, in the end, only 705 passengers and crew would be saved.

***

Although the orders were to put women and children first into the lifeboats, most people probably do not know that more males were saved than females when the final tally of survivors was made. In some cases, men were put into the boats to reassure reluctant women that they were safe to board. In other cases, male members of the crew were ordered into the boats to ensure that they were properly manned by seasoned sailors.

However, as a percentage of passengers, the majority of men on board *Titanic* perished when she slipped below the surface of the frigid North Atlantic in the early hours of 15 April. A review of the statistics shows that only 20 per cent of the men on board survived the sinking, compared to 74.35 per cent of the women. Then again, one must consider that there were many more men on board than women. Still, it is an interesting fact that more men than women survived – a fact many do not realise.

The Twelfth Circumstance
The Coal Strike that Increased the Death Toll

In January 1912, coal miners in Britain had gone on strike for higher pay. As a result, supplies of coal used to fuel ships became increasingly difficult to obtain. As the strike wore on, more and more ships were taken out of service. The White Star Line even made an announcement that the speed of *Olympic* and *Titanic* would be dropped from 23 knots to 20 knots to save coal.

The strike finally ended on 6 April 1912, but not in time to get newly mined coal to the docks before *Titanic*'s maiden voyage. In order to lift the speed limitations placed on *Titanic*, White Star Line would have to take coal from other ships it owned that were docked in Southampton. These included the *Majestic*, *Adriatic* and *Oceanic*. Since that would put those ships out of service, White Star had to make other travel arrangements for their passengers and many of those headed for New York were transferred to the *Titanic*.

Also out of service because of the strike and docked at Southampton were the *St Louis, New York, St Paul* and the *Philadelphia* of the American Line. Coal from these ships and some of their passengers were also moved to *Titanic*.

Most of the affected passengers saw the transfer as a stroke of good luck, as accommodations aboard the *Titanic* were generally far superior to those of the ships on which they originally had been booked. Second-class accommodations on some of those other ships were not as pleasant as third class aboard the *Titanic* – so the transfers were considered good fortune indeed.

71

As *The Shipping News* wrote in its 14 June 1911 issue about *Titanic*'s sister ship *Olympic*, these new liners set a new standard for luxury:

> The Second Class and Third Class are furnished in a style that represents, without exaggeration, what was thought sufficient for the First Class only a few short years ago; and if there is one thing more than another that should induce Second and Third Class travelers to patronise this great liner, it is the fact that they share in all the advantages of an absolutely steady, practically unsinkable ship with those who can afford the highest-priced suite of rooms that the *Olympic* can boast. This is a consideration of the first importance to all who are in the least afraid of the sea.
>
> But it is when we reach the public rooms that we best realise what the large vessel means. She is a floating palace; and in three or four of the principal rooms there is nothing to distinguish them from the rooms of some stately country house or elegantly furnished hotel on the sea front. It is difficult to believe we are afloat.

The coal strike also affected the crew members employed by the idled liners, with an estimated 17,000 out of work because of the cancelled sailings. Accordingly, they too turned to *Titanic* when it came time to hire the crew for her maiden voyage. There were long lines at the White Star's office as those unemployed by the circumstances hoped for assignments to join the most luxurious liner of the time. Neither they, nor the passengers they would serve, had any inkling of the tragedy that lay ahead of them.

In effect, the labour dispute by striking coal miners would have the unintended consequence of increasing the *Titanic*'s death toll.

The Thirteenth Circumstance
Deadly Secrets

Perhaps the most disturbing accusations about *Titanic*'s design being faulty came from Tom McCluskie, a former long-term employee of Harland & Wolff who worked both in its shipyard and its engineering offices. Eventually, he found himself in charge of the company's archives and its millions of pages of drawings, plans, files, notes and photographs – including the notebooks of Thomas Andrews, the man who had been the chief designer of *Olympic* and *Titanic*.

Clearly, the loss of the *Titanic* reflected badly on Harland & Wolff – and any indication that its design and construction was responsible for her sinking would have exposed it to lawsuits that would have easily bankrupted the company, as well as her affiliate, the International Mercantile Marine headed by J.P. Morgan. As McCluskie revealed in his book *The Rise and Fall of Harland and Wolff*, 'this resulted in an unspoken but rigidly enforced policy never to publicly discuss the ship afterwards.' So the company made sure that all of the documents related to *Titanic* were locked away.

According to McCluskie, the company doubled down on this policy in 1955 following publication of Walter Lord's best-selling book *A Night to Remember*, which detailed the liner's last night – and renewed great interest in the ship and the disaster after years of waning attention. Soon, Harland & Wolff found itself with a flurry of requests seeking information about *Titanic*, so the company took a new tack. It simply responded that all of the documentation had been destroyed during the Second World War when Belfast had been bombed in April and May 1941. It was a lie, but no one challenged it – until Tom McCluskie finally revealed the truth years later.

In the mid-1990s, Harland & Wolff had agreed to let McCluskie serve as a paid technical adviser to James Cameron's movie *Titanic*. By now, the old Harland & Wolff had disappeared, having been sold to a Norwegian shipping company after years of being kept afloat by subsidies from the British government. The rule of secrecy about the *Titanic* had slowly evaporated and McCluskie's access to knowledge made him a celebrity among *Titanic* buffs, but not enough to draw the attention of those now running the company. Eventually that would change and McCluskie's activities would result in management's distaste for his reminding the world that Harland & Wolff had created something that had claimed over 1,500 lives. Clearly, the company did not see it as a point of pride and McCluskie's relationship with the front office soured.

In 1997, two days after a particularly nasty battle with the head of the company, McCluskie suffered a stroke that left him unable to work. He received half pay from the company for six months, but then his disability benefit ended. With that, McCluskie turned to what he knew best – writing books about Harland & Wolff and the ships it had built, including *Titanic* and *Olympic*. Still, he did not reveal the greatest secret of all about what he knew.

Although he was enjoying some success as a writer, McCluskie longed for his old job and, by 2000, he felt well enough to return to Harland & Wolff. But his request to go back to work was flat out refused. He was only 50 years old but the company told him to take his pension and be done with it.

More years would pass as McCluskie continued to shoulder the burden of knowing the secret of *Titanic*'s fatal flaw. Then he decided to contact Roger Long, a marine architect and researcher.

Long had spent many years digging into the *Titanic* tragedy and was one of the notable few who had seen the wreck first-hand. He was fortunate to be one of the three crew members aboard one of the

Mir submersible missions that had ventured the two miles below the surface of the North Atlantic to *Titanic*'s final resting place.

In 2005, he was now part of a team that was working to decipher why *Titanic* appeared to be so weak that it had broken up as she was sinking. McCluskie knew he had the answer and he approached Long to reveal it. With the lingering effects of the stroke dogging him, McCluskie knew every day could be his last and he did not want to take the secret he knew to the grave.

***

Although frail, Tom McCluskie ventured from Belfast to the Woods Hole Oceanographic Institute located on the southern tip of Cape Cod. With a camera crew ready to capture what he had to say, McCluskie sat before Roger Long and began sharing what he had learned during the hundreds of hours he had spent in the Harland & Wolff archives. What he revealed would change everything.

In reading Thomas Andrews' notes about the *Olympic*, McCluskie had found that Andrews was startled when he saw the ship's hull 'panting' during its sea trials – flexing ever so slightly as it moved through the water, but still visible to the eye. While Andrews had designed the ship to flex to some extent in response to the effect of waves against the hull, this seemed excessive.

He wrote his concern about the *Olympic* in his notebook, although he knew it was too late to do anything about it. Yet, Andrews was concerned that his hull design was not stiff enough, so he would try to rectify it before *Titanic* and the third sister, *Britannic,* were put into service.

Back at Harland & Wolff, Andrews ordered the addition of steel reinforcement to the area between the *Titanic*'s double bottom and its hull, as well as steel bracing that would enclose the promenade deck. The latter change was visibly noticeable, but White Star said it was simply done to provide space for a small restaurant, as well as to protect passengers from any sea spray that might be carried up by the wind. In short, it was just a cover story and one of many secrets that would be kept quiet for decades to come.

Andrews' fears about the *Olympic*'s hull were confirmed when she was dry-docked after her collision with the *Hawke*. During repairs to the ship's damaged hull, an inspection revealed that both her hull plates and rivets had developed cracks because of the flexing. The discovery was one of many McCluskie had found hidden away in the Harland & Wolff archives. His revelations were beginning to lift the fog that had long covered the reasons why *Titanic* had been torn apart as she sank – but his big reveal was still to come.

***

Even before Andrews' design of the *Olympic*-class liners was completed, the Harland & Wolff archives showed that one of his key decisions had been overridden by White Star President, Bruce Ismay.

Andrews' notes clearly indicated that he had originally specified the hulls of the massive White Star liners be built with 1¼-inch steel plates. His calculations had convinced him this was the size needed to provide his ships with acceptable strength. However, Ismay disagreed and demanded the ships be built lighter, likely to reduce both construction costs and the amount of fuel needed to move them through the water.

Andrews defended his decision, but eventually acquiesced. After all, Ismay was footing the bill and the customer was always right. Instead, Andrews reworked his design to use 1-inch steel instead, reducing *Titanic*'s weight by half a million pounds.

But the change would result in the launch of ships with much less tolerance for stress, especially if a portion of the ship flooded and lost its buoyancy. The deadweight would pull ever more downward against the rest of the hull and would become more pronounced as more of the ship flooded – just as would happen with *Titanic*. As the bottom wreckage would later confirm, the forces had become too much for the keel and the bottom plates to resist. Eventually this lighter-weight steel would snap apart and speed the ship's demise.

In fact, according to McCluskie, Harland & Wolff's own internal investigation into the disaster had led the company to believe that *Titanic* had broken up while still on the surface. It also convinced Edward Wilding, the man who would replace Andrews, to believe she might have floated longer or even survived had she been built stronger.

Unfortunately, the circumstances which led to this fatal flaw – and the ultimate effect they had on *Titanic*'s strength and safety – never came out publicly in either the American or British inquiries that were held soon after her sinking. The officials asking the questions simply did not think to ask, nor did they have any reason to think Harland & Wolff would deliberately compromise the design and construction of its ships. And Harland & Wolff was certainly not about to volunteer such information and completely undermine public confidence in the company and its products.

But within weeks after its internal review of the wreck, *Titanic*'s sister ship *Olympic* was brought back to Harland & Wolff to receive a massive retrofit that would seek to correct the flaws that sunk the 'unsinkable' White Star Liner. The upgrades would include installing a partial double hull and raising many of the bulkheads to make them truly watertight. *Britannic* would undergo similar improvements as she sat unfinished in the yard. To no one's surprise, *Olympic* was also outfitted with enough lifeboats to evacuate every person on board.

But it was too little – and much too late – to save the great *Titanic*. In the end, it turned out that design flaws, substandard materials manufactured by less skilled workers, and a refusal to build a stronger hull had all combined to produce yet another round of circumstances that would contribute to *Titanic*'s untimely end.

The Fourteenth Circumstance
Questions of Confusion, Panic and Mistakes on the Bridge

There was another long-kept secret that may have played a role in *Titanic*'s loss. It finally came to light when the granddaughter of Second Officer Charles Lightoller claimed he had talked about a possible fatal mistake that he believed contributed to the disaster. According to Louise Patten, her grandfather revealed that confusion over rudder orders had caused 'an officer to steer into an iceberg instead of away.'

Calling it a dark family secret, Patten claimed in an article carried by London's *Daily Express* on 31 October 2011 that her grandmother had been told by Lightoller:

> First Officer William Murdoch was on watch when he saw
> a large iceberg ahead. He ordered the helmsman Robert
> Hitchins (actually spelled Hichens) to 'hard a starboard'
> to sail round the iceberg. Remarkably Hitchins steered in
> the wrong direction.

Although Patten was born two years after Lightoller died, she said her grandmother had often talked to her about the *Titanic* and what she had learned about the disaster from her husband.

Patten claimed there was a second part to the secret: that Bruce Ismay, chairman of the White Star Line, who was on board at the time, ordered Captain Smith to keep *Titanic* moving despite its damaged hull so as not to delay the ship's arrival in New York. After the collision, the engine room was ordered to proceed 'Ahead Slow' for a while until it was discovered the ship was too badly damaged to continue. But according to Lightoller, this led the ship to sink many hours earlier than it might have otherwise because the ship's forward movement forced more water into the damaged hull.

> My grandmother told me my grandfather was always very gentle about Hitchins, as he believed he made an honest mistake. However, he remained angry about Ismay's decision which he believed resulted in the huge loss of life.

However, there is concern about the veracity of the Lightoller story. At the time of the collision, he was in his cabin, not on the bridge. Patten says he heard second hand about the steering mistake – and Ismay's command to proceed – from his colleagues as he and the other senior officers prepared evacuation of the ship.

Lightoller himself barely survived the disaster, being blown clear of the sinking ship by a blast of air that broke him free from the grate he was pinned against by water rushing into the ship. Hours later he and the other survivors were picked up by the rescue ship *Carpathia*. Once aboard, Patten says Lightoller was ordered to go to a cabin occupied by Ismay.

'It was then the cover-up was planned,' she said in the newspaper article. 'Ismay told my grandfather that if he told the full story of the steering blunder and Ismay's decision to keep the damaged ship moving, White Star's insurance would be invalidated. The firm would be bankrupted and every single employee and sailor would lose their job,' Patten said.

When Lightoller later appeared before the two official government inquiries into the sinking, he did not reveal what he had heard from any of his fellow senior officers after the collision.

'Rightly or wrongly, my grandfather decided that his first duty was to protect his employer and his fellow employees, and in his autobiography, he made it clear that this was exactly what he had done,' Patten explained.

***

Not only was *Titanic* the pride of the White Star Line, so was her master, Captain Edward John Smith. Since 1904, Smith had been the Commodore of the White Star Line and was responsible for overseeing its flagships. He was seen as a strong and knowledgeable captain and, as such, had developed a loyal following of passengers who would specifically book a passage on whatever ship he was commanding. Eventually, he became known as the 'Millionaire's Captain' – attracting a clientele made up of the era's most rich and famous.

Smith's career was mostly without incident. As Commodore, White Star had given him command of its grandest ships when each came into service. Among them was the *Baltic*, the largest ship in the world at the time she first sailed. Her maiden voyage from Liverpool to New York began on 29 June 1904 and went without incident. Soon after, Smith took control of his second new 'big ship,' the *Adriatic*. Again, the maiden voyage was uneventful. Eventually, Smith was handed the *Olympic* in 1911 – the largest moving object in the world until *Titanic* launched the following year. But with *Olympic*, Smith's luck would begin to change.

On 21 June 1911, as *Olympic* completed her maiden voyage from Southampton, she was pulling into New York's Pier 59 assisted by a dozen tug boats. Suddenly, one of the tugs became trapped under the giant liner's stern after backwash from her propellers spun the tug around and sucked it under. Fortunately, it was able to break free and limp to safety.

Olympic would be involved in a much more serious accident the following September when its great size would once again work against her. This time, as previously described in this book, the British warship *Hawke* would be sucked into her stern. The collision punched a sizeable hole in the *Olympic* and left the *Hawke* with a crumbled bow. Yet neither of these incidents would affect Smith's reputation or cause him much concern. In fact, the accident with the *Hawke* likely further convinced Smith – as it did many others – that the modern ships under his command could overcome any adversity.

During his career, Smith had said more than once that he was confident in the safety of sea travel. Interviewed in 1906, he said: 'I cannot imagine any ship which would cause a ship to founder. I cannot conceive of any vital disaster happening to this vessel. Modern shipbuilding has gone beyond that.'

He followed this in 1907, stating:

> When anyone asks me how I can best describe my experiences of nearly 40 years at sea, I merely say 'uneventful'. I have never been in an accident of any sort worth speaking about. I never saw a wreck and have never been wrecked, nor was I ever in any predicament that threatened to end in disaster of any sort.

Clearly, Smith had never faced an emergency like the one presented to him aboard *Titanic* the night of 14 April 1912. And stories regarding his conduct following the collision with the iceberg raised questions as to how well he took control of the situation.

In fact, the official inquiry held by the U.S. Senate concluded *Titanic*'s Captain Edward Smith had shown an 'indifference to danger [that] was one of the direct and contributing causes of this unnecessary tragedy.'

The British Inquiry also held Smith responsible, but to a lesser degree, finding that he had followed the standard practice of not taking action to slow down or alter course until it was clear that danger was imminent. Lord Mersey, who headed the British investigation, stated:

> He [Smith] made a mistake, a very grievous mistake, but one in which, in the face of the practice and of past experience, negligence cannot be said to have had any part; and in the absence of negligence, it is, in my opinion, impossible to fix Captain Smith with blame.

As both inquiries found, there was no doubt that Smith failed to reduce *Titanic*'s speed, although he had clearly received numerous warnings about dangerous ice ahead. In addition to the custom of maintaining full speed until danger was obviously present, perhaps he also thought there would be plenty of time to see anything that was big enough to sink a ship the size of *Titanic* – especially since the weather was calm and clear.

However, there is some firm evidence that Smith's leadership and reaction to the disaster did not seem to live up to his reputation.

First, he decided to leave the bridge during a crucial time during the voyage – at night and just prior to entering an area where ice had been reported.

Second, once the collision occurred, it appears Smith never fully informed all of his officers of the severity of the situation. For instance, Quartermaster George Rowe, stationed on the Poop Deck at the rear of the ship, had no idea that the decision had been made to evacuate the ship. He phoned the bridge to ask why he had just seen a lifeboat go past.

Third – and perhaps the sharpest criticism of Smith's performance after the collision – he allowed lifeboats to leave the ship less than fully loaded. Even though there was not enough room for everyone, another 500 lives could have been saved had each lifeboat taken its full capacity.

Some critics believe Smith became panicked and indecisive. However, in his defence, it can be assumed that once he gave his officers and crew orders to prepare the boats and begin evacuating the passengers, Smith would have relied on his ship's organisational structure to carry out his commands. In other words, his officers and the crew under them would have the actual responsibility to follow through and get the job done. Having delegated the work, Smith would have mostly done his part to manage the situation.

Still, he was the captain, and as such, he bore ultimate responsibility for his ship and the wellbeing of his passengers.

***

According to several eyewitnesses, Smith took time to check on the progress being made to evacuate the ship, including at least one trip to the radio room to follow up on whether there had been any success reaching a ship that could arrive before *Titanic* sank. As the end neared, he released members of the crew, telling them it was time to save themselves.

Smith's final moments aboard *Titanic* are uncertain and will never be known for sure. Several sources say he was seen on the bridge at 2.13 am, just seven minutes before the ship sank. James McGann, one of the ship's firemen who survived the wreck, later claimed he had been with Captain Smith on the bridge a few minutes before water swept over the wheelhouse.

'I was helping to get off a collapsible boat,' McGann was quoted as saying. 'The last one launched when the water began to break over the bridge on which Captain Smith stood. When the water reached Captain Smith's knees, and the last boat was at least 20 feet away from the ship, I was standing beside him.

'He gave one look all around, his face firm and his lips hard set. He looked as if he was trying to keep back the tears, as he thought of the doomed ship. I felt mightily like crying as I looked at him.

'Suddenly, he shouted: "Well boys, you've done your duty and done it well. I ask no more of you. I release you. You know the rule of the sea. It's every man for himself now, and God bless you".'

Smith apparently observed another rule of the sea – that the captain goes down with his ship. Smith disappeared with *Titanic* and his body was never found.

Above left: In 1898, a full fourteen years before the *Titanic* tragedy, Morgan Robertson writes his book *Futility*. The story is about a British passenger ship sailing the North Atlantic in April when it hits an iceberg and sinks with great loss of life. His story is eerily similar to what will actually happen to *Titanic* in April 1912. (Author's collection)

Above right: Lord Pirrie of Harland & Wolff (L) and Bruce Ismay of the White Star Line (R), inspect *Titanic* prior to her launch. Their dinner in 1907 would lead to the creation of the largest and most luxurious ships of their time. (Robert Welch, Harland & Wolff official photographer (Public domain))

Work on *Titanic*'s keel begins on 31 March 1909 at Harland & Wolff 's yard in Belfast. Her hull will take over a year to finish and another ten months to complete once her hull is launched. (Robert Welch, Harland & Wolff official photographer (Public domain))

Yard workers use a giant hydraulic riveting machine to secure *Titanic*'s hull plates. This is the preferred construction method, but the size of the machinery makes it impossible to use in the ship's narrower spaces. (Robert Welch, Harland & Wolff official photographer (Public domain))

Riveters working in confined spaces within the ship are forced to manually install rivets using brute force with sledgehammers. These rivets are less sturdy than those installed using hydraulic equipment. When *Titanic* strikes the iceberg, most of the damage occurs in areas where rivets were manually installed. In addition, the rivets included large amount of 'slag' which made them brittle in cold temperatures. (Robert Welch, Harland & Wolff official photographer (Public domain)

Olympic and *Titanic* sit side by side at Harland & Wolff surrounded by the massive Arrol Gantry built especially for their construction. *Olympic* is painted light grey so she will photograph better in black and white. Her hull will be repainted black before her launch on 20 October 1910. (Robert Welch, Harland & Wolff official photographer (Public domain))

Harland & Wolff Head Foreman, Robert Keith, stands by the hydraulic lever that will release the *Titanic* for launch, allowing her to slide down the slipway and into the water. (Robert Welch, Harland & Wolff official photographer (Public domain))

Titanic just after her launch on 31 May 1911. It will take another ten months to complete her superstructure and interior. (Robert Welch, Harland & Wolff official photographer (Public domain))

Although *Titanic*'s rudder was 78 feet high and weighed about 101 tons, it was considered to be slightly small for the ship's size. It was made even less effective when the propellers were reversed after the iceberg was spotted. As a result, it failed to turn the ship in time to avoid the collision. (Robert Welch, Harland & Wolff official photographer (Public domain))

Titanic's purser Hugh McElroy (left) with Captain Edward Smith (right) stop for a photograph. Both men will perish in the disaster. (Reverend Francis Patrick Browne (Public domain))

Olympic (left) is being manoeuvred into dry dock in Belfast for repairs on the morning of 2 March 1912 after losing a propeller blade. *Titanic* (right) is moored at the fitting-out dock. It is the last time the two ships are ever photographed together. (Robert Welch, Harland & Wolff official photographer (Public domain))

Titanic is guided by tugs as she prepares to undergo her sea trials early on the morning of 2 April 1912. Her fitting out had been completed just two days before. Aboard were seventy-eight stokers, greasers and firemen, and forty-one crew members. Over the course of twelve hours, *Titanic* runs at different speeds and her turning ability is tested. A 'crash stop' is also performed with her engines fully reversed. It takes 3 minutes and 15 seconds, and 850 yards for her to stop. When the iceberg is spotted on the night of 14 April, it is just 37 seconds ahead. (U.S. National Archives and Records Administration (Public domain))

Titanic leaves Southampton shortly after noon on 10 April 1912 as she heads for her next port of call: Cherbourg, France. (Joseph H. Bailey (Public domain))

Moments after leaving her Southampton berth, *Titanic*'s massive displacement snaps the mooring lines of the *New York* and pulls her toward *Titanic*'s stern. The near-miss nearly ends the maiden voyage. (Reverend Francis Patrick Browne (Public domain))

The last known photo of *Titanic* afloat, taken on 11 April 1912 off the coast of Ireland. There are an estimated 2,224 souls aboard – but lifeboats for only 1,178. (Reverend Francis Patrick Browne (Public domain))

Titanic's first-class passengers enjoy the most opulent ocean liner ever built, as represented by her grand staircase. Even third-class passengers find their accommodations equal to those of second class found on other ships. (Robert Welch, Harland & Wolff official photographer (Public domain))

Among those aboard *Titanic*'s maiden voyage was Thomas Andrews, the man who designed her. Credit: The National Archives (Public domain)

The first ice warning received by *Titanic* on the morning of 14 April 1912. The *Coronia* reports 'Captain, Titanic – West-bound steamers report bergs, growlers and field ice in 42° N, from 49° to 51° W, April 12th. Compliments, Barr'. Captain Smith posts the message on the bridge to inform his officers. (British Wreck Commissioner's Inquiry (Public domain))

Members of *Titanic*'s crew turn out for a life jacket inspection. Although the lifeboats only have capacity for about half of those on board, there are enough life jackets for everyone. But they will offer no protection against the freezing cold of the North Atlantic waters. (Reverend Francis Patrick Browne (Public domain))

The fifth and final ice warning to *Titanic* from *Mesaba*. It is received at 9.40 pm and warns there is dangerous ice directly in the path of the ship: 'From Mesaba to Titanic. In latitude 42° N to 41° 25, longitude 49° W to longitude 50° 30W, saw much heavy pack ice and great number large icebergs, also field ice, weather good, clear.' But it is never taken to the bridge by radio operator Jack Phillips because it does not carry the prefix 'MSG' signifying it is a message for the captain. Phillips puts the message aside and continues sending passenger messages to Cape Race. Two hours later, *Titanic* strikes the iceberg. (British Wreck Commissioner's Inquiry)

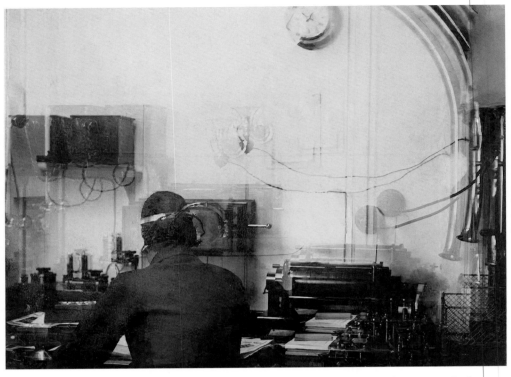

The only known photo of *Titanic*'s wireless room with Marconi operator Jack Phillips at the set. The photo was taken by Father Francis Browne who sailed from Southampton to Queenstown, his ticket a gift from his uncle. An American couple he met on board offered to pay his way to New York but when he telegraphed his superior for permission, he received a curt 'GET OFF THAT SHIP'. (Reverend Francis Patrick Browne (Public domain))

Titanic lookout Frederick Fleet, who spotted the fatal iceberg. He calls the bridge and famously yells 'Iceberg, right ahead', but it is too late – the iceberg is just 37 seconds ahead. Fleet survives the sinking and returns to sea on other vessels but finds *Titanic* crew members are shunned. In 1965, following the death of his wife, he is depressed, despondent and broke, and hangs himself. (Wikipedia, unknown author (Public domain))

Русское Восточно-Азіатское Пароходство.

The Russian East Asiatic S. S. Co. Radio-Telegram.

S. S. Birma

No.	Words	Origin. Station.	Time handed in	Via.	Remarks.
69.		*Titanic*	11·55" april 14=15		Distress Call sigs loud

Cqd - SOS. from *M.G.Y*
We have struck iceberg sinking
fast come to our assistance
Position Lat 41·46 N. Lon 50·14 W
M.G.Y

L. L. Cannon
2.0 W.d.

Ships all over the North Atlantic hear *Titanic*'s call for help, among them Joseph Cannon, a newly-qualified wireless operator aboard the *Birma* (call sign SBA). Cannon works for Marconi's rival, The United Wireless Company, which has ordered its operators to offer no assistance to Marconi-equipped ships. Cannon ignores this order and informs his captain. Cannon replies to *Titanic*: 'We are 100 miles from you steaming 14 knots. Be with you by 6.30. Our position lat. 40.48N, long. 52.13W. SBA.' Unfortunately, *Birma* is too far – and too slow – to be of help. (British Wreck Commissioner's Inquiry (Public domain))

Form No. 1—100—18.5.11.

The Marconi International Marine Communication Company, Ltd.

WATERGATE HOUSE, YORK BUILDINGS, ADELPHI, LONDON, W.C.

COPY.

To: Commander *Titanic*

Am lighting up all possible boilers as fast as can
Haddock

Titanic's sister *Olympic* messages she is coming to her assistance – 'Lighting up all possible boilers as fast as can' – but she is some 580 miles away. After *Titanic* sinks, she offers to take survivors from the *Carpathia,* but the offer is declined. *Carpathia*'s Captain, Arthur Rostron, fears the sight of *Titanic*'s twin will upset those who had escaped the wreck. (British Wreck Commissioner's Inquiry (Public domain))

R.M.S. "CARPATHIA"

Rescue ship *Carpathia* normally runs at just 14 knots, but her captain orders all possible steam diverted to her engines as she races to *Titanic*'s aid. Heat and hot water are turned off and she reaches a speed of 17 knots as her passengers awaken to find their cabins have gone cold. (Wikipedia, unknown author (Public domain))

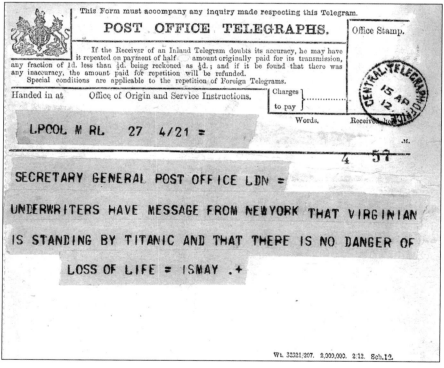

This Form must accompany any inquiry made respecting this Telegram.

POST OFFICE TELEGRAPHS.

Office Stamp.

If the Receiver of an Inland Telegram doubts its accuracy, he may have it repeated on payment of half amount originally paid for its transmission, any fraction of 1d. less than ½d. being reckoned as ½d.; and if it be found that there was any inaccuracy, the amount paid for repetition will be refunded. Special conditions are applicable to the repetition of Foreign Telegrams.

Handed in at   Office of Origin and Service Instructions.   Charges to pay ....

Words.   Received here

LPCOL M RL   27   4/21 =

4   57

SECRETARY GENERAL POST OFFICE LDN =

UNDERWRITERS HAVE MESSAGE FROM NEWYORK THAT VIRGINIAN

IS STANDING BY TITANIC AND THAT THERE IS NO DANGER OF

LOSS OF LIFE = ISMAY .+

Wt. 32321/207. 2,000,000. 2/12. Sch.12.

Confusion reigns during the early hours of the disaster. Many newspapers erroneously report that all of *Titanic*'s passengers have been saved and that the stricken ship is being towed to Halifax by the line *Virginian*. In reality, it is a broken-down oil tanker that is under tow, but wireless operators misunderstand the message and assume it is the *Titanic* that is being rescued. (British Wreck Commissioner's Inquiry (Public domain))

The partially flooded Collapsible Lifeboat D pulls towards *Carpathia* at 7.15 am. It was the last boat to be successfully launched before *Titanic* sank. Credit: Wikipedia, unknown author (Public domain)

With an additional 705 people on board the *Carpathia*, space is tight. Many survivors spend some time on deck bundled up against the cold as the ship makes her return to New York. Credit: Smithsonian Institution, unknown author (Public domain)

Bruce Ismay's Marconigram sent from the *Carpathia* to the White Star Office in New York: 'Deeply regret advise you Titanic sank this morning fifteenth after collision iceberg, resulting serious loss life; further particulars later.' (Published by RMS *Carpathia*)

Headlines around the world scream the news of *Titanic*'s sinking and the great loss of life. With full information slow in coming, many of the initial stories are based on conjecture and rumour. (*New York American*, 16 April 1912)

Titanic's junior wireless operator, Harold Bride, his feet frostbitten, is helped off the *Carpathia* after she docks in New York. He is met by Guglielmo Marconi and a reporter from *The New York Times*, who offers him $1,000 for his story. (Wikipedia, unknown author (Public domain))

With events happening so quickly, *The New York Times* is unable to pull an advertisement promoting *Titanic*'s planned return trip to England on 20 April. (*The New York Times*, 1912)

Above left: J. Bruce Ismay, hand on his chin, is the first witness called to testify at the U.S. Senate inquiry held at the Waldorf Astoria Hotel in New York. Vilified by the press for saving himself, the tragedy will haunt him for the rest of his life. (Library of Congress, unknown author (Public domain))

Above right: Within a month of the sinking, the movie *Saved from the Titanic* is released to take advantage of the public's intrigue with the tragedy. It is co-written by and stars popular actress of the day Dorothy Gibson, herself a *Titanic* survivor. (Éclair Film Company, 1912)

The 'Unsinkable' Margaret 'Molly' Brown presents *Carpathia* Captain Arthur Rostron with an award for his service. After helping others evacuate the *Titanic*, she boarded lifeboat 6 and took an oar to help row. She pleaded to return to the debris field to look for survivors but was unsuccessful, with the crew of the boat fearing it would be swamped by panicked people in the water. (Library of Congress, George Grantham Bain (Public domain))

Memorials to the victims of *Titanic* were erected around the world. In Belfast, where she was built, this monument was funded by contributions from the public, shipyard workers, and victims' families. It was dedicated in June 1920. (Wikipedia, Man Vyi (Public domain))

The author with survivor Millvina Dean at a *Titanic* conference in Springfield, Massachusetts on 18 April 1998. Millvina was only two months old and travelling to America in third class with her mother, father and brother when the ship struck the iceberg. Sensing something was wrong, her father quickly got his family on deck and into a lifeboat. Sadly, he would not survive. (Author's collection)

The Final Circumstances
Bits of Good Fortune

There were, however, a few notable instances in which circumstances just happened to bring unforeseen *good* fortune to a handful connected to *Titanic*.

One involved the American millionaire J.P. Morgan, the man who actually controlled the White Star Line through the holdings of his International Mercantile Marine Company – known as the IMM. Morgan had been on hand for the launch of *Titanic* in 1911 and he had booked passage on her maiden voyage. But, at the last moment, he cancelled his trip to stay in France. The decision allowed him to escape the certain death suffered by *Titanic*'s other millionaire passengers.

Chocolate magnate Milton Hershey and his wife also missed *Titanic*'s inaugural trip when business concerns interrupted their travel plans, calling them back early to his company's Pennsylvania headquarters. Instead of boarding the new liner, they decided to book passage on the *Amerika* – the very ship that would ask *Titanic* to relay its warning about the deadly ice that lay directly in her path.

There were a handful of lesser-known others who missed the sailing as well. One of those was Annie Jordan, a resident of Lack in County Mayo, Ireland. At the last minute, she cancelled her third-class ticket due to a facial rash.

The anonymous holder of ticket 242154 also changed plans. He or she was given a full refund by the White Star ticket office just prior to *Titanic*'s departure.

Circumstances involving a case of bad timing – or perhaps good timing – would also save three *Titanic* crew members from the disaster. The episode was later related by passenger Lawrence Beesley, who watched what happened as he stood on deck along the ship's rail.

The trio had decided to duck ashore for a final pint of ale before the sailing, but found their way back blocked as the last 'boat train' chugged its way off the dock after depositing its passengers. After the train's last car had passed, the men ran to the gangplank, but they were deemed late and denied re-entry to the ship. Only days later, as news of *Titanic*'s loss swept throughout her home port, did the would-be crew members come to see that their misfortune had actually been a blessing.

Perhaps the most ironic circumstance of good fortune befell Guglielmo Marconi, his wife and children. Marconi – whose very radio equipment was credited with saving so many lives after the disaster – had been offered free passage on *Titanic*, along with his family. Instead, he had taken Cunard's *Lusitania* three days earlier so he could attend to urgent business in New York. As his daughter Degna later explained, her father also had paperwork to do and preferred the public stenographer who worked aboard the Cunard vessel.

Marconi decided he would have to delay his enjoyment of *Titanic*'s many fine amenities and luxuries until he boarded her for the return trip from New York to England. However, he left in place the plans for his wife and children to make *Titanic*'s maiden voyage so that they could enjoy the thrill of being aboard.

Marconi's wife, Beatrice, 4-year-old daughter Degna and his infant son, Giulio, were preparing to board the new White Star liner when fate again intervened. Just prior to *Titanic*'s scheduled sailing on 10 April, little Giulio came down with what was termed 'baby fever.' The attending physician prohibited the little boy from travelling until he was better and the trip was cancelled. On the day the great ship sailed out of Southampton, Beatrice and Degna watched from the riverside as she sailed past in all her splendour without them.

One can only conjecture what would have happened to Marconi and his family had they sailed aboard *Titanic* as they had originally planned. Would the order of 'women and children first' have left the great inventor aboard the slanting deck of the sinking ship as his wife and children were lowered away in a lifeboat? After all, that was the fate of many other rich and famous men that night, including millionaires John Jacob Astor IV, Benjamin Guggenheim and Isador Straus.

Given the stature of the many men who perished that night, the evidence suggests Marconi's position and fame probably would not have saved his life had he been aboard.

***

It was also by circumstance, premonition and plain luck that the wife and children of another family were saved, despite the fact they were far from being rich or well known. That was the family of Elizabeth Gladys 'Millvina' Dean, who would become *Titanic*'s last living survivor.

I had the honour of meeting her in April 1998 at the annual convention of the Titanic Historical Society held in Springfield, Massachusetts. She had travelled to the event from her home in Southampton, England – the very place from where *Titanic* had started her maiden voyage. At the time, I was working as a broadcast journalist for WNYT, the NBC television affiliate in Albany, New York, a 90-minute drive from Springfield. I had done a series of stories regarding the *Titanic*'s ties to the Albany area (including several local residents who had been aboard during the maiden voyage), so the opportunity to meet Dean gave me ample reason to make the trip.

Millvina was just a 2-month-old baby and the youngest person aboard when *Titanic* sank. She was also the last survivor to die, passing away on 31 May 2009. Even though she was far too young to have any personal recollection of that night, I found her story fascinating, her wits sharp and her demeanour gracious. As I interviewed her, even at the age of 86, she clearly remembered how her mother had told her as a little girl how she came to be on the ship – and how she, her mother and brother were saved. It was all because her father had the foresight to lead them to lifeboat 10 soon after the ship had struck the berg.

'My father had perished in the wreck and now, some seven years later, my mother was going to be remarried,' Millvina told me as we sat together in her hotel room. 'She wanted me to know what had happened to my father, and why she was taking a new husband.

'She told me that my father had felt the ship hit the iceberg and that he immediately realised something was terribly wrong because the engines had stopped,' she began. 'Even though no one else seemed to share his sense of worry, he felt we needed to get up on deck right away.

'He told my mother to get us kids bundled up and then he took us out of the lower part of the ship where our third-class cabin was located. He wasted no time taking us up the stairs to the main deck where lifeboats were. It was still early and it turned out that most people were still reluctant to get into a lifeboat and leave the nice warm ship. So when a sailor told him to put my mother, my brother and me in the lifeboat, my father didn't hesitate.'

Then, with a look of sadness, she said, 'He wasn't allowed to go and he tried to reassure my mother that he would get away in another boat just as soon as all of the women and children on board were taken care of. Then my parents waved goodbye to each other as the boat was lowered away. It was the last time she ever saw him.' Bertram Frank Dean was only 25 when he died that night. His body was never recovered.

In another bit of irony, the Dean family was among those who were never supposed to be aboard *Titanic* in the first place. They had originally booked passage on White Star's *Adriatic*, but because of the coal strike that had crippled England in 1912, their booking was cancelled. Both they – and *Adriatic*'s coal – would instead be transferred to the new pride of the White Star fleet.

The Dean family had been on their way to Wichita, Kansas, where the family had relatives and a tobacco shop. Millvina's father had been offered co-ownership in the business, so he decided to make a new life for his family in America, just like millions of other immigrants.

To be transferred to the *Titanic* seemed to bode well for his decision, as their third-class accommodations aboard her were far superior to those found on most other ships, including the *Adriatic*. Better yet, they would not have to pay anything extra to ride the new elegant liner! The cost of their ticket, number 2315, would remain at 20 pounds 11 shillings and 6 pence. Still, it was a good deal of money for an English working-class family in 1912.

The death of Bert Dean would, of course, change Millvina's life forever. After the disaster, her widowed mother decided to take the family back to England. Millvina often talked about how she should have grown up in America and reflected on how different her life might have been. Yet she always gave thanks to the father she never knew, whose premonition and quick thinking saved her and the rest of her family. After all, three-quarters of her fellow third-class passengers died in the sinking.

But most ironic of all was the fact that her death, on 31 May 2009, came exactly ninety-eight years to the day that *Titanic* had been launched from the Harland & Wolff yard in Belfast. In a fitting last wish, she was cremated and, on 24 October 2009, her ashes were scattered around the very dock in Southampton from which the *Titanic* had set sail.

Her death marked the last living link to the world's greatest maritime disaster. She was also the last person who had survived because – unlike so many others – circumstances had fortunately lined up in her favour.

Titanic: The Aftermath

The Numbers

- 31.6% – percentage of people aboard (passengers and crew) who survived the sinking.
- 53.4% – percentage who could have survived, if all of the available lifeboat spaces had been filled.
- 492 – the number of *Titanic* passengers who survived (not including crew).
- 37% – percentage of passengers who survived.
- 61% – percentage of first-class passengers who survived.
- 42% – percentage of second-class passengers who survived.
- 24% – percentage of third-class passengers who survived.
- 109 – the total number of children on *Titanic*.
- 56 – the number of children who survived.
- 52 – the number of children in third class who died.
- 2 – the number of dogs to have survived (both were small lapdogs taken by their owners into lifeboats).
- 20% – percentage of male passengers who survived.
- 75% – percentage of female passengers who survived.
- 214 – the number of *Titanic* crew members who survived.
- 24% – percentage of crew members who survived.
- 22% – percentage of male crew members who survived.
- 87% – percentage of female crew members who survived.
- 50% – percentage of Navigation Officers who survived (there were eight aboard).
- 0% – percentage of Engineering Officers who survived (all twenty-five died while working to keep the *Titanic* afloat for as long as possible after the collision).

- 100% – percentage of lookouts who survived.
- 13 years, 5 months, 26 days – the age of the youngest female survivor from first class, Lucile Polk Carter.
- 11 months, 8 days – the age of the youngest male survivor from first class, Hudson Trevor Allison.
- 64 years, 8 months, 8 days – the age of the oldest female survivor from first class, Mrs Mary Eliza Compton (also the oldest survivor overall).
- 60 years, 6 months, 21 days – the age of the oldest male survivor from first class, Mr Maximilian Josef Frölicher-Stehli.
- 10 months, 22 days – the age of the youngest female survivor from second class, Barbara Joyce West.
- 7 months, 17 days – the age of the youngest male survivor from second class, Viljo Unto Johannes Hämäläinen.
- 59 years, 8 months, 30 days – the age of the oldest female survivor from second class, Mrs Lutie Davis Parrish.
- 62 years, 1 month – the approximate age of the oldest male survivor from second class, Mr George Harris (exact birthday unknown).
- 2 months, 13 days – the age of the youngest survivor from third class, Elizabeth Gladys 'Millvina' Dean (also the youngest survivor).
- 5 months, 7 days – the age of the youngest male survivor from third class, As'ad Tannūs.
- 63 years, 10 months, 9 days – the age of the oldest female survivor from third class, Mrs Hedwig Turkula.
- 45 years, 8 months, 24 days – the age of the oldest male survivor from third class, Mr Charles Edward Dahl.

***

The *Mackay-Bennett*

Within hours of *Titanic*'s loss, the White Star Line began the process of recovering the bodies of the more than 1,500 victims. The gruesome task fell to the *Mackay-Bennett,* a cable-laying ship berthed at Halifax, Nova Scotia. She was chosen because she had a cargo hold capable of storing the 125 coffins and the ice that would be needed to preserve any bodies recovered.

The owners and crew of the ship were further motivated by Joseph Astor's offer to pay a $100,000 reward to the ship that recovered the body of his father, J. J. Astor.

The *Mackay-Bennett's* captain, Frederick Larnder, prepared for the job by setting his ship up to become a mobile mortuary, adding aboard both specialised personnel and supplies needed for the assignment. Among them was the chief embalmer of Nova Scotia's largest undertaking firm. To entice the crew to help with the morose work, they were offered twice their regular pay.

On 17 April, two days after *Titanic's* sinking, the *Mackay-Bennett* left Halifax about 12.30 pm and started the 900-mile trip to the wreck site. It would take four days to complete, slowed by both heavy fogs and rough seas.

In the meantime, the crew prepared for the 'class based' recovery plan that had been created: first-class passengers were to be embalmed and placed in coffins; those from second class were to be wrapped in linen sheets and placed on ice; third-class bodies were to be weighted down and buried at sea.

Early on the morning of 20 April, the *Mackay-Bennett* anchored close to the spot where *Titanic* had sunk and lowered the skiff lifeboats that would be used to pick up the bodies of *Titanic's* victims. Crews then rowed into the recovery area to bring aboard as many bodies as they could safely handle for the trip back to the ship. On their first trip, they picked up a total of fifty-one corpses. But it soon appeared that there would not be enough space or embalming supplies – especially because Canadian regulations required all bodies to be treated before being allowed into the country.

Among those recovered was the wealthiest man who had been aboard the ill-fated liner – first-class passenger John Jacob Astor.

Although his body had begun to decompose, he was identified by the unique diamond ring he wore, as well as by the initials sewn on the label of his jacket.

Also brought aboard was the body of *Titanic*'s band leader, Wallace Hartley, his music case still strapped to his body. His remains would be transferred to the *Arabic* and returned to England where he would be buried in mid-May.

Meanwhile, 116 bodies deemed to be those of third-class passengers were weighted down and buried at sea. Of these, only fifty-six were able to be identified.

The *Mackay-Bennett* would remain at *Titanic*'s grave site until just past midnight on 26 April. After spending a week working on recovery operations, she headed back to Halifax with 190 bodies, including the remains of an unidentified third-class infant boy.

As promised, Joseph Astor paid the $100,000 he had offered for the recovery of his father's body. The crew of the *Mackay-Bennett* chose to share the money, with each receiving approximately $2500.

To properly bury the infant boy who had been recovered, the crew used some of Astor's money to cover the cost of the child's funeral, casket and headstone. The casket was marked with a simple copper plaque inscribed with '*Our Babe.*' On 4 May, every member of the *Mackay-Bennett*'s crew turned out at Fairview Cemetery in Halifax for the infant's internment – joined by a large crowd of local residents touched by the little boy's tragic death.

One of those residents, Clifford Crease, would visit the child's grave every year on the anniversary of the *Titanic*'s loss. When he passed away in 1955, he was buried a few feet away from the child known only as '*Our Babe.*'

For 95 years, the name of the child remained a mystery but, in 2007, his true identity was finally discovered. Using modern technology, Canadian researchers at Lakehead University announced that testing of the toddler's DNA revealed who he was: 19-month-old Sidney

Leslie Goodwin. Like so many others who perished with the *Titanic,* he had been travelling with the rest of his family to start a new life in America – a new life that would never take place.

***

The *Olympic*

As would be expected, the *Titanic* disaster had an immediate impact on the White Star Line and her sister *Olympic.* She, too, was not equipped with lifeboats for everyone on board, so White Star hurriedly cobbled together a collection of second-hand collapsible lifeboats and stuffed them aboard as soon as she returned to Southampton, laying them three deep on her decks. But although the company was determined to keep *Olympic* in service, passenger bookings fell off sharply.

On 24 April 1912 – just ten days after *Titanic* hit the iceberg – *Olympic* was due to sail at noon for New York with a thousand fewer passengers than had been aboard *Titanic*'s maiden voyage. But 20 minutes before the scheduled departure, several firemen declared that the forty collapsible boats placed aboard the ship were rotten and not seaworthy. Word quickly spread among others in the crew and a demand was made for the collapsibles to be replaced with regular wooden lifeboats.

The confrontation was soon in the lap of Philip Curry, White Star's Southampton manager. He tried to subdue the brewing mutiny by reassuring the men that the forty collapsible boats had been approved by a Board of Trade inspector, adding that it would be impossible in any event to swap the suspect craft because of the time constraints. Curry's pleas swayed no one.

Within minutes, the entire crew of firemen, greasers, and trimmers – some 276 in all – deserted their posts, singing 'We're All Going the Same Way Home' accompanied by a tin whistle band under the direction of a self-appointed conductor. For an hour, the dock was a scene of bedlam. Many of the strikers who had walked off the job soon appeared to be intoxicated, and blocked those trying to board the ship. A hastily called meeting of the Seafarers' Union assembled on the dock and its Secretary, A. H. Cannon, called for a strike vote. Scores of hands went up, with not a single man voting to rejoin the ship.

In defending his union members, Canon told *The New York Times*:

> The men inspected the boats when they were mustered this morning and found many of them in a rotten condition. One man is alleged to have put his hand through the canvas of one boat. All the boats are from six to ten years old, and when the men tried to open them, they could not do so. Further, only four extra men had been signed on to man the boats.

A union member chimed in, saying: 'What we demand is that every one of the lifeboats shall be a wooden one. Personally, I do not care, as I am unmarried, but many of the men have wives and families, and their lives are as valuable as those of the first-class passengers.'

Meanwhile, White Star was able to pull together a skeleton crew from some of its other liners, with rumours of them being offered extra pay if they would join *Olympic*. Finally, she managed to sail away from the turmoil around 2.00 pm. But without enough engine room hands to adequately run her boilers, she only got as far as Spithead off the Isle of Wight before stopping and dropping anchor.

In an effort to reassure *Olympic*'s crew and get the ship underway again, it was decided to test the seaworthiness of the suspect collapsible boats. Four were chosen by the Seafarers' Union and lowered into the water.

'We agreed to test four of the collapsible boats selected by us,' said Councillor T. Lewis, President of the Union. 'We tested the boats in water for three hours and passed three as seaworthy, though one of the three was leaking slightly. The fourth boat had a hole in her and was leaking badly. We agreed that she was unseaworthy, and afterward told Mr Curry, the Southampton Manager of the White Star Line, and Capt. Haddock, the Commander of the *Olympic*, that we were prepared to recommend the men to return if the unseaworthy boat was replaced. These terms were accepted.'

Still, the situation remained unresolved. By now, White Star had managed to find a group of non-union workers to replace the strikers, but the union members aboard the ship loudly objected and refused to work with the newcomers. The stranded passengers – some of whom had passed the time flying kites from the ship's deck – were now growing more impatient with the impasse. A group even volunteered to work in the stokehold.

'Our idea,' said passenger Ralph Sweet, 'was that we should stoke the boat to Queenstown, where the Captain would have been able to get fresh men. About a hundred passengers volunteered altogether, and we would have been able to work in short watches. Capt. Haddock thanked us very nicely, and I thought he was going to put us to work right away, but he told us afterward that he would not call on our services.'

Another effort was undertaken by the Duke of Sutherland, who was also travelling aboard. He tried to raise a crew of volunteer yachtsmen, but found it was impossible to fill the places of all the deserters. During all of this, another 300 passengers who were to board at Cherbourg, France, found themselves taken off tenders and sent to hotels to await the outcome of the dispute.

Olympic's woes were soon being picked up by newspapers on both sides of the Atlantic. *The New York Times*, which had first broken the news of *Titanic*'s demise, carried a series of stories on the situation. And, as news of the ship's dilemma spread, sightseers took to hundreds of small boats to look on as the *Olympic* sat motionless. Undeterred, White Star continued its efforts to get her trip to New York under way.

But the firemen who had walked off the job made one more demand – the discharge of the seventeen stokers who had remained on board the ship and loyal to the company. White Star refused and said it would cancel *Olympic*'s voyage before it would give in to firing those who had stood by the firm. It was soon clear that attempts to staff the engine room were failing at every turn.

Finally, on the evening of 26 April, the *Olympic* abandoned her trip to New York and returned that evening to Southampton, where the passengers disembarked about 8.00 pm. White Star refunded the passengers' money and decided to lay up the ship until at least 15 May while it worked to resolve the issue with the lifeboats. Her passengers found themselves scurrying to locate another way to New York, with many rushing to catch Cunard's *Lusitania*, which was set to leave Liverpool the following day.

In response to the strike by *Olympic*'s firemen, White Star called for their prosecution as mutineers. The managers of the line sent a telegram to Britain's Postmaster-General, stating the circumstances under which they had been compelled to abandon the voyage and expressed the hope that there would be official support to secure proper punishment for the crew's 'mutinous behaviour.'

Shortly afterwards, the strikers found themselves being arraigned in Southampton's Police Court. It was a classic battle between management and labour, and the magistrates found themselves in the middle. Brief testimony was taken as to the circumstances surrounding the event, but the case was held over and no action was taken against the men.

In early May, *The New York Times* reported the outcome of the dispute in a brief story: 'PORTSMOUTH, 4 May – The seamen of the White Star liner *Olympic*, who quit that vessel after the strike of the firemen were allowed to go to-day by the magistrates sitting in the police court here, where the men were tried on a charge of mutiny. The magistrates decided that the charges were proved against the fifty-four mutineers, but expressed the opinion that it would be inexpedient to imprison or fine the defendants under the circumstances which had arisen prior to their refusal to obey orders. The magistrates discharged the defendants and hoped they would return to duty.'

Olympic finally returned to regular service in mid-May but by the autumn, it was clear White Star needed to do something to restore faith in its giant liner. On 9 October 1912, White Star resigned itself to the inevitable and withdrew *Olympic* from service. The liner would be returned to Belfast, where her builders – Harland & Wolff – would heavily modify the ship to improve her overall safety, incorporating the many lessons learned from the *Titanic* disaster.

The long list of improvements included increasing the number of lifeboats carried by *Olympic* from twenty to sixty-eight. In addition, extra davits were installed along the boat deck to accommodate them. The boiler and engine rooms were also reconstructed and given an inner watertight skin that, in effect, created a double hull. The same modification would also be performed on the yet-to-be-launched *Britannic*.

Attention was also given to one of the biggest deficiencies that helped to sink the *Titanic* – the shortened bulkheads that allowed water to flow from one compartment to the next after she hit the iceberg. Five of those bulkheads were extended up to B Deck, raising them to the entire height of the hull. This corrected a flaw in the original design where the bulkheads only rose up as far as E or D Deck, placing them only a few feet above the waterline.

To further improve safety, an extra bulkhead was added to subdivide the electrical dynamo room, increasing the total number of watertight compartments from sixteen to seventeen. Additional improvements were made to the ship's pumping equipment. After *Titanic* began to flood, her crew found it impossible to stay ahead of the inrushing water, partly because her pumps were located too far aft.

Once completed, the modifications meant that *Olympic* could survive a collision similar to the one that doomed *Titanic*. Now, the ship's first six compartments could be breached and she could remain afloat. By contrast, *Titanic* was only designed to survive with her first four compartments flooded – and she could not survive when five were breached in the collision with the iceberg.

At the same time, *Olympic*'s B Deck also underwent a refit, adding a number of additional amenities for passengers' comfort. These included extra cabins, more private bathing facilities and a Café Parisien (which had proved popular on *Titanic*), offering another dining option to her first-class passengers.

With these changes – followed by a second refit in 1919 after she returned from service as a First World War troop carrier – *Olympic*'s gross register tonnage rose to 46,439 tons, making her 111 tons bigger than *Titanic*.

In March 1913, the newly renovated *Olympic* returned to passenger service and briefly regained the title of largest ocean liner in the world. But she would only hold this title for three months. In June 1913, the German liner SS *Imperator* entered passenger service at 52,117 gross registered tonnage.

Following *Olympic*'s refit, White Star launched a major marketing campaign calling her the 'New *Olympic*' and touting her improved safety features prominently in advertisements. The travelling public responded and bookings improved.

Despite the horrible tragedy that befell her sister, *Olympic* would enjoy a long career spanning twenty-four years from 1911 to 1935. Her reputation was bolstered during her service as a troopship, earning her the nickname, 'Old Reliable.' In fact, during conversion back to commercial service in 1919, she was dry-docked and a dent with a crack was discovered below her waterline in the centre of her hull. A further investigation concluded it had been caused during the war by a German U-boat torpedo that had failed to detonate.

After her post-war refit, *Olympic* once again returned to civilian service and enjoyed a successful life as a transatlantic liner throughout the 1920s and into the first half of the 1930s. Her best year was 1921, when she carried a record number of 38,000 passengers on the transatlantic route.

As the memory of *Titanic* faded, *Olympic* attracted celebrities of the day. Her passenger list included Marie Curie and Charlie Chaplin. On a July 1920 voyage, Mary Pickford and Douglas Fairbanks would celebrate their honeymoon aboard. Also on that trip was a then-unknown 16-year-old named Archibald Leach – who would later become famous as Cary Grant.

Although her 1919 refit had also converted her from burning coal to oil – reducing re-fuelling from days to hours and engine room personnel from 350 to 60 – *Olympic* could not keep up with the competition she faced from more modern liners. Her days would be further numbered by the slump in trade brought about by the Great Depression, which cut transatlantic passenger traffic by half.

Adding to her downfall was a decision by the United States to begin restricting immigration in 1924. This had been much of *Olympic*'s bread and butter, but the change now forced her to trade European immigrants for third-class tourists instead. Competition became fierce for travellers who desired comfort without the usual high ticket prices.

During 1933 and 1934, *Olympic* ran at a net operating loss for the first time. The worst year was 1933, when she carried a total of just over 9,000 passengers. Bookings rose slightly in 1934, but many of her Atlantic crossings still lost money.

With her operation becoming increasingly unprofitable, it was decided by Cunard-White Star (the two competitors had merged in 1934) that *Olympic* would be retired after her final transatlantic trip from New York on 5 April 1935. The company briefly considered using her as a summer cruise ship but soon dropped the idea. This was followed by a group of investors who proposed turning her into a floating hotel off the coast of France. This idea also failed to materialise.

On 11 October 1935, *Olympic* left Southampton for the last time and sailed to the scrappers. Her fittings were sold off first and then her superstructure was demolished. By the end of 1937, the breakers had finished with *Olympic*'s hull and *Titanic*'s sister was no more.

By the time the end came for *Olympic*, she had completed a total of 257 round trips across the Atlantic, transporting 430,000 passengers on her commercial voyages, and travelling a total of 1,800,000 miles. In addition, during her admirable wartime service, she was reported to have carried some 201,000 troops and war personnel, burning 347,000 tons of coal in the process and travelling another 184,000 miles.

No one doubted she had proven herself well worthy of her nickname – 'Old Reliable.'

***

The *Britannic*

Although always denied by both the White Star Line and shipbuilder Harland & Wolff, a rumour has long persisted that *Britannic* – the third sister of the *Olympic*-class liners – was originally to be named *Gigantic*. According to the tale, after the *Titanic* disaster the name was dropped by White Star to avoid the appearance of arrogance.

However, it has been claimed that in early 1911 some American newspaper stories referenced that a ship by that name had been ordered by White Star. A poster was also said to be published with a ship named *Gigantic* on it, but it did not carry the White Star name or logo, unlike the company's official marketing materials. British maritime archives and the records of Harland & Wolff have also never been found to contain any reference to that name.

Although *Olympic* and *Titanic* had been named early on, the third sister was only referenced as '433', her keel number. However, by October 1911, Harland & Wolff's records show that the name *Britannic* had been assigned. But like many rumours, this one refuses to die.

Unlike her two sisters, *Britannic* would be built but never enter commercial service. As she was still under construction when the

First World War broke out, she would be requisitioned by the British government and converted to serve as a hospital ship.

Following the *Titanic's* loss, *Britannic's* original dimensions and plans were altered to include the safety modifications that would also be incorporated into the *Olympic*. This included widening her beam from 92 to 94 feet to accommodate the addition of a double hull. Bulkheads were also raised to make her compartments truly watertight. Now, she, too, would be capable of floating with her first six compartments flooded.

There would also be additional lifesaving equipment installed. These would include five large electrically-powered davits on the deck, each capable of launching six lifeboats which were stored on gantries. These would replace the manually-operated Welin davits that were on *Titanic* and *Olympic*.

Britannic's new davit system meant additional lifeboats could be stored on the deck house roof and still be reached for launching. The new gantry davits could also reach lifeboats on the other side of the ship, allowing them to be launched, even if the ship developed a list that would normally prevent lifeboats from being lowered. However, several of these davits were placed directly across from the ship's funnels, with the unintended consequence of actually defeating the original purpose.

In all, *Britannic* would carry forty-eight lifeboats and these would be larger than those on her sisters – each capable of carrying at least seventy-five people, as opposed to the sixty-five on the others. While *Britannic* would be capable of carrying 3,309 passengers and crew, the improved lifeboat system meant at least 3,600 people could be accommodated in the event of the need to abandon ship.

The changes would bring her to a total of 48,158 gross tons, making her bigger than both her sisters, but not the largest ship in service by the time she was launched. That record had already been taken over by the German liner SS *Vaterland*.

While still in her slipway, the First World War had begun and work on *Britannic* slowed as men and materials were diverted to wartime needs. By May 1915, tests of her engines had been completed and the British Admiralty was informed that she could be prepared for emergency service with just four weeks' notice. That same month, a German U-boat torpedoed and sank Cunard's RMS *Lusitania* near the Irish coast, further escalating hostilities.

To protect the Suez Canal – a vital route for Allied supplies – landings had begun on the Gallipoli Peninsula, but these proved to be disastrous for the Allies and the casualties mounted. It was soon clear that there was a need for large hospital ships to treat and evacuate wounded soldiers. *Britannic* would get the call to serve on 13 November 1915.

To prepare her for wartime service, *Britannic* was repainted white and large crosses were placed on her sides along with green stripes. She was also given a new name – HMHS *Britannic* (His Majesty's Hospital Ship). Her luxury passenger spaces were also renovated to include some 3,300 beds and several operating rooms. Common areas of the upper decks were transformed into rooms for the wounded and the cabins on B Deck were set up as accommodations for doctors. Both the first-class dining and reception rooms on D Deck were converted into operating rooms as well.

On 12 December, she was pronounced ready and two weeks later set sail for the island of Lemnos in the Aegean Sea to bring back wounded soldiers. She would make five such trips in all, but the sixth would bring about her premature end.

On 21 November 1916, a loud explosion shook the ship shortly after 8.00 am. *Britannic* had struck an underwater mine in the Kea Channel that had been planted the month before by German submarine *U-73*. The extent of the damage was soon apparent – and grim.

The blast on the ship's starboard side was now quickly flooding the first four compartments – and water was also finding its way into boiler room six, coming down the tunnel that connected it to the firemen's quarters located in the bow. To make matters worse, the watertight door between boiler rooms five and six was jammed open. Still, with the improvements made after the *Titanic* disaster – including higher bulkheads – *Britannic* should have been able to withstand the damage and remain afloat. But human error would defeat those safeguards.

Despite standing orders to keep the ship's portholes closed, nurses had opened many of them to allow fresh air into the wards. As the flooding sea pulled the ship's bow down, water began pouring through those openings and into the aft portion of the vessel. In just ten minutes, *Britannic* was roughly in the same condition as the *Titanic* had been in one hour after striking the iceberg. *Britannic* would soon reach her flood limit.

As *Britannic* was within sight of the island of Kea, Captain Charles Bartlett decided he would try to beach the ship to save her. But the blast had knocked out the ship's steering mechanism, making it difficult to manoeuvre. He tried using the engines to turn the ship, but found she was slow to respond. In the meantime, two lifeboats were prematurely launched and ripped to shreds by the still-turning propellers, killing several of those trying to escape.

Finally, Bartlett realised the ship was sinking too rapidly to reach shore and ordered its evacuation. As the bridge slipped underwater, the captain and his assistant commander simply stepped off into water and swam to a nearby lifeboat. Of the 1,065 people on board, 1,035 would survive.

Britannic, the largest ship lost in the First World War, sank in 400 feet of water at 9.07 am. In spite of the many safety improvements made to her after *Titanic*'s demise, *Britannic* had remained afloat just 55 minutes after the explosion.

***

White Star Chairman, J. Bruce Ismay

The *Titanic* disaster changed the life of Bruce Ismay, White Star Chairman, forever. The once mighty visionary of the company fell into shame and disfavour almost as soon as he stepped into collapsible lifeboat C as *Titanic* slipped below the North Atlantic. Within days of the sinking, newspapers on both sides of the Atlantic were calling him J. 'Brute' Ismay and the 'Coward of the *Titanic*' – fiercely condemning him for seeking refuge while hundreds of others died in icy waters. The Hearst Newspapers – well known at the time for so-called 'yellow journalism' – vilified Ismay at every opportunity. It published lists of all those who died, but in the column of those saved, it had just one name: Ismay.

But Ismay was clearly shaken by the tragedy. Once aboard the rescue ship, *Carpathia*, he went to the cabin of the ship's doctor. During the entire voyage to New York, he never left the cabin and never ate. The doctor kept him sedated with opiates.

One survivor of the wreck, 17-year-old Jack Thayer, even tried to console him – despite having lost his father in the sinking. He later recalled his meeting with Ismay in the doctor's cabin: '[Ismay] was staring straight ahead, shaking like a leaf. Even when I spoke to him, he paid absolutely no attention. I have never seen a man so completely wrecked.'

Ismay only reluctantly tried to defend his actions, telling both the American and British inquiries that he only entered the lifeboat when he was sure that no more women and children were on hand to be saved. He seemed more comfortable letting others come to his defence, including the British Board of Trade. In its final report on the *Titanic* tragedy, it stated:

> Mr Ismay, after rendering assistance to many passengers, found 'C' collapsible, the last boat on the starboard side, actually being lowered. No other people were there at the time. There was room for him and he jumped in. Had he not jumped in he would merely have added one more life – namely, his own – to the number of those lost.

Another male passenger in the boat, William Carter, also said that there was no one else around when he and Ismay got in the boat. However, Carter's own behaviour and reliability was criticised by his wife, who claimed he had left her and their children to fend for themselves after the collision. She sued Carter for divorce in 1914, accusing him of 'cruel and barbarous treatment and indignities to the person.'

Despite Ismay's hope that his situation in accessing a lifeboat would be understood, he would continue to live under *Titanic*'s cloud for the rest of his life. He found that London society ostracised him and considered him a coward. On 30 June 1913, he resigned as chairman of the White Star Line.

Though cleared of blame by the official British Inquiry, Ismay would never recover, keeping a low profile afterwards. He lived part of the year in a large cottage he owned in County Galway, Ireland. Although no longer involved in passenger shipping, he continued to be active in business, with much of his attention focused on the insurance company founded by his father, The Liverpool & London Steamship Protection & Indemnity Association Limited. He also donated large sums of money to maritime organisations, including a fund to assist families of lost seamen.

However, his wife would seek to protect him from *Titanic*. Florence Ismay forbade her family from discussing the tragedy. Ismay's granddaughter, Pauline Matarasso, likened her grandfather to a 'corpse' in his later years:

> Having had the misfortune (one might say the misjudgment) to survive – a fact he recognised despairingly within hours – he withdrew into a silence in which his wife made herself complicit, imposing it on the family circle and thus ensuring that the subject of the *Titanic* was as effectively frozen as the bodies recovered from the sea.

Ismay also had a residence in London, where he would attend concerts at St George's Hall or occasionally take in a movie – almost always by himself. Sometimes he would venture into a park and strike up a conversation with a complete stranger. But those who knew him well said he continually contemplated the *Titanic* tragedy. One friend said he 'tormented himself with useless speculation as to how the disaster could possibly have been avoided.'

Although his wife tried to shield him from the disaster, one of his grandsons brought it up during a family gathering at Christmas in 1936. When the boy learned that his grandfather had been involved in shipping, he asked if he had ever been shipwrecked. Ismay finally broke his quarter-century silence on the tragedy: 'Yes, I was once in a ship which was believed to be unsinkable.'

Bruce Ismay would only live another year, having been diagnosed with diabetes which required his right leg to be amputated. On 14 October 1937, he suffered a massive stroke and collapsed at his London home. Three days later, he died at the age of 74, his death coming at almost the same time as *Olympic*'s final demolition.

***

Californian Captain Stanley Lord

The *Titanic* tragedy would also haunt another man for the rest of his life – Stanley Lord, Captain of the *Californian*. Initially, the world knew nothing of the *Californian*'s role in the disaster. After she learned of the *Titanic*'s sinking from the *Carpathia* the morning after the wreck, she had briefly helped to search the scene and then proceeded on to Boston.

On 22 April, the hastily called U.S. Senate investigation learned that a ship had been near the *Titanic* but had failed to respond to her distress signals. However, the identity of the ship was not immediately known.

The next day, *The Clinton Daily Item*, a small Massachusetts newspaper, carried an appalling story that claimed the *Californian* had refused to come to the aid of the sinking White Star liner. The story quoted James McGregor, the *Californian's* carpenter, who stated that his ship had been close enough to see *Titanic's* lights and distress rockets. The *Californian* was further implicated by a story in the *Boston American* the same day. The source for that article was the ship's assistant engineer, Ernest Gill, who essentially told the same story as McGregor. Lord was immediately vilified for not coming to *Titanic's* aid.

Within days, Lord found himself subpoenaed to appear before the U.S. Senate hearing, along with members of his crew, including Gill.

Lord originally stated that there was another ship about 4 miles away, but he was convinced it was not the *Titanic*. Lord believed it was an illegal fishing vessel (often referred to as the 'Mystery Ship') and that *Titanic* was at least 20 miles away. As such, he believed the slow speed of his ship would not have allowed him to reach the sinking White Star liner in time to render any meaningful assistance. Unfortunately for Lord, his testimony was inconsistent and sometimes conflicted with itself. Meanwhile, what Gill told the investigators was solid and unwavering. Lord's insistence that a third ship was in the area was also rejected during the testimony of Captain J. Knapp of the U.S. Navy Hydrographer's Office. Knapp made it clear that *Titanic* and *Californian* were in sight of each other and that no third vessel had been in the area that night.

On the night of *Titanic's* loss, Lord explained he had stopped the *Californian* for the night after coming across a large field of ice. He had asked his wireless operator, Cyril Evans, to warn other ships of the danger and, as noted earlier in this book, Evans contacted *Titanic* but was rudely cut off by her wireless operator, Jack Phillips, who was busy sending messages to Cape Race. Soon after, Evans shut down his set and went to bed for the night.

Members of *Californian's* crew admitted to the Senate panel they had seen a number of white rockets fired in the distance and twice they called Lord in his cabin to advise him. Lord assumed they were 'company rockets' which were used by ships to identify themselves to other vessels operated by the same company. However, it was revealed that Lord never took action to wake the ship's wireless operator to learn what was happening. An attempt was made by the *Californian* to make contact using its Morse lamp, but her crew could not make out any response. They came to believe the flickering light they saw in the distance was simply the mast light of the other ship.

Neither the American nor British inquiries did anything to dispel the criticism that was heaped upon Lord and his crew. In fact, both were critical of Lord but stopped short of recommending he be criminally charged. Unfortunately, when Lord was called to testify, he was not given the opportunity to be represented by counsel, or to defend himself with rebuttal testimony. The American inquiry stung Lord particularly hard, stating: 'such conduct, whether arising from indifference or gross carelessness, is most reprehensible, and places upon the commander the *Californian* a grave responsibility.'

In the end, Lord's reputation was badly damaged and he found himself shunned by the public and other mariners alike. His career was also damaged with his employer – the Leyland Line – which fired him in August 1912. It would be six months before he would find himself back at work, taking a job with the Nitrate Producers Steamship Company after getting help from a Leyland director who felt he had been treated unfairly.

Lord would retire from the sea in 1937 because of health reasons, but he would never cease his efforts to clear his name in the *Titanic* disaster. Twenty years later, Lord approached the Mercantile Marine Service Association in Liverpool to ask for help. Its General Secretary, Leslie Harrison, agreed to assist and petitioned the Board of Trade on his behalf for a re-examination of the facts. By the time Lord died in 1962, a decision in the matter had still not been reached.

Three years later, in 1965, Lord's petition was formally rejected because he had not offered any new evidence to exonerate himself. This was followed by a second petition in 1968, which was also rejected. Although Lord never lived to see his reputation restored, his son, Stanley Tutton Lord, continued to fight for his father up until his own death in 1994.

The discovery of *Titanic*'s wreck in 1985 once again turned a spotlight on Lord and the *Californian*. The location of the wreck revealed that the last position given by the *Titanic* was some 13 miles from where it was actually found. This offered new evidence that perhaps the *Californian* was, in fact, too far away to offer assistance to the sinking ship. As a result of this new information, many came to believe the *Californian* could not have reached *Titanic* any faster than the *Carpathia* was able to arrive.

However, an informal review published in 1992 by the British government's Marine Accident Investigation Branch (MAIB), further faulted Lord's inaction. Among its conclusions was that although the *Californian* was likely out of visual sight of the *Titanic*, the distress rockets she sent up had easily been seen by the *Californian*'s crew. This report, too, was critical of *Californian*'s officers and Lord for not reacting to the signals. Of course, the still unanswered question is why Lord did not simply wake his radio operator and listen for any distress signals.

In death, as in life, Captain Stanley Lord's name remains tarnished and much of the true story of the *Californian* is still wrapped in conjecture and mystery.

***

Carpathia Captain Arthur Rostron

The experience of *Carpathia*'s Captain Arthur Rostron would become the complete opposite of Stanley Lord's. Following his rescue of *Titanic*'s 705 survivors, Rostron was showered with praise for his remarkable efforts to reach the stricken liner before she slipped below the surface of the North Atlantic.

Among the honours he received was the Congressional Gold Medal from the United States Congress, and appointment as a Knight

Commander of the Order of the British Empire. His employer, Cunard, also recognised his outstanding service, eventually promoting him to Commodore of the Cunard fleet.

Rostron was relatively new to the *Carpathia* when he took command of her on 18 January 1912 – just four months before the *Titanic* tragedy. But he didn't hesitate for a moment when word reached him from the ship's wireless operator that the new White Star liner had hit an iceberg and needed immediate assistance. As his ship made its way over the 58 miles to *Titanic*'s reported location, Rostron ensured that everything was prepared and in good order to rescue survivors.

In all, he issued some two dozen orders to be carried out by *Carpathia*'s crew, leaving nothing to chance. Excerpts from an interview with Rostron after the disaster tell the story first-hand:

> When in chart-room working out the position and course, I saw the boatswain's mate pass with the watch as they were going to wash down the decks. I called him and told him to knock off all work, and get all our boats ready for lowering, and not to make any noise; also that the men need not get excited, as we were going to another vessel in distress.
>
> I had already sent for the chief engineer, and on coming up told him to turn out another watch of stokers and make all speed possible and not to spare anything, as we were going up to *Titanic*, she being in trouble, having struck ice. The chief engineer hurried away at once, and I then sent for [the] English doctor, purser and chief steward. These officers were soon in my cabin, and I related the circumstances and gave the following instructions:
>
> • English doctor, with assistants, to remain in the first-class dining-room; Italian doctor in second, and

Hungarian doctor in the third-class dining-room, and to have a supply of stimulants, restoratives and everything necessary.

- Purser, with assistant purser and chief steward to receive the people at the different gangways, controlling our own stewards in assisting the *Titanic*'s people to the dining-rooms, etc.
- Also, get Christian and surnames of survivors as soon as possible to send by wireless.
- Inspector, steerage stewards, and masters-at-arms to control our own steerage passengers and keep them out of third-class dining-hall, also to keep them out of the way, and off the deck, to prevent confusion.
- Chief Steward that all hands would be called, and to have coffee, etc., ready to serve out to our men. Have coffee, tea, soup, etc., in each dining-room for rescued. Have blankets near gangways, in saloons and public rooms, and also some handy for our own boats.
- To see all rescued cared for and immediate wants attended to, that my cabin and all officials' cabins would be given up for accommodation of rescued; smoke-rooms, libraries, and dining-rooms, if necessary, to be utilised as accommodation.
- All spare berths in steerage to be used for *Titanic*'s Third class, and to get all our own steerage passengers grouped together.
- To all, I strictly enjoined silence, order, and strict discipline; also to station a steward in each alleyway to reassure our own passengers should they inquire about any noise they might hear.
- After receiving their instructions, these officers hurried away to make their preparations.

I then went on to the bridge, and soon after the Marconi operator came up and reported he had picked up a message from *Titanic* to *Olympic*, asking the latter to have all his boats ready. But previous to this the operator had received a message from *Titanic*, asking when we would be up there. I told him to reply: 'About four hours.' We did it in less than three and a half hours. I told the operator to inform *Titanic* all our boats would be in readiness, and also all preparations necessary.

After the operator left, I gave the following instructions to the first officer:

- All hands to be called and get coffee, etc.
- Prepare and swing out all boats; all gangway doors to be opened.
- Electric clusters at each gangway and over the side A block – with line rove – hooked in each gangway.
- A chair – slung – at each gangway for getting sick or wounded up.
- Pilot ladders and side ladders at gangways and over the side.
- Cargo falls, with both ends clear and bight secured, along ship's side on deck, for boat ropes or to help people up.
- Heaving lines and gaskets distributed about the decks and gangways, to be handy for lashings, etc.
- Forward derricks rigged and topped, and steam on winches – to get mails on board or as required.
- Pour oil down forward lavatories, both sides, to quiet the sea.
- Canvas ash-bags near the gangways to haul the children up in.
- Ordered company's rockets to be fired from 3.00 am, and every quarter of an hour, to reassure *Titanic*.
- Also arranged as to how the officers would work, should the situation require the service of our boats.

About 2.35 am, the doctor came on the bridge and reported all my instructions carried out, and everything in readiness.

From now on, we were passing bergs on either side and had to alter course several times to keep well clear of them. You may depend on it, we were keyed up pretty tight, and keeping a bright lookout. I was also fully aware of our danger, knowing what had already occurred to the *Titanic*. So it can be imagined I was pretty anxious, thinking of my own passengers and crew and ship, as well as those on the *Titanic*.

We had three and a half rushing, anxious hours, and plenty to think of and plenty to do in the meantime in order to be ready. We started sending up rockets at intervals of about a quarter of an hour, and when nearer fired the company's Roman candles (night signals), to let them know it was *Carpathia*.

About 4.00 am, I stopped the engines, knowing we must be somewhere near the position. A few minutes after, I saw an iceberg right ahead, and immediately the Second Officer reported the same.

We had seen the green flare light low down not long before, and so knew it must be a boat. I had intended taking the boat on the port side, which was the lee side if anything, but with the iceberg to consider, I swung the ship around and made to pick up the boat on the starboard side. Another few minutes and the boat was alongside... and found her to contain about twenty-five people, and in charge of an officer.

Now comes the heart-rending part when we knew for a certainty the *Titanic* had gone down; I sent word to the gangway to ask the officer to come up to me on the bridge when he came aboard.

On coming up to the bridge, I shook hands and asked: 'The *Titanic* has gone down, I suppose?'

'Yes,' he replied – but what-a-sad-hearted 'Yes' it was – 'she went down about two thirty.'

As daylight broke, Rostron and his crew could see the immense ice field *Carpathia* had somehow safely ventured into. He told a junior officer on the bridge to count the number of bergs that were at least 200 feet high. The tally estimated at least twenty-five to be from 200 to 250 feet high – and dozens of bergs from 50 to 150 feet high. Nothing less than a miracle had got *Carpathia* through this deadly swathe.

By 8.00 am, all of *Titanic*'s lifeboats and the survivors they carried had been brought aboard. Captain Rostron arranged to hold a short service near to the spot where the great liner had sunk. Held in the first-class dining room, it offered a short prayer of thankfulness for those saved and a short service for those lost.

After consulting with Bruce Ismay, it was decided to bring *Titanic*'s 705 survivors to New York, their original destination. Rostron turned his ship around but found the trip slowed by heavy thunderstorms and fog early on the morning of Tuesday, 16 April. *Carpathia* finally arrived in New York on the evening of Thursday, 18 April as heavy rain fell. Before berthing at the Cunard Pier, Rostron brought his ship to Pier 59, the White Star Pier where *Titanic* had been scheduled to arrive. There, he ordered the lost ship's lifeboats lowered and rowed to her still waiting berth.

Upon landing at *Carpathia*'s own berth, Rostron, his crew and passengers found themselves deluged by relatives of the survivors, throngs of the curious and dozens of reporters. The next morning's newspapers would be emblazoned with headlines and first-hand stories about the survivor's ordeals, the rescue – and, of course – the heroic actions of Captain Rostron and *Carpathia*.

Despite the high praise given to Rostron, he was not one to keep it all for himself. In his follow-up report to Cunard's management, he offered recognition, thanks and gratitude to his crew members for their efficiency and professionalism.

Rostron was also deeply religious and he publicly acknowledged that he was guided the night of the sinking by a higher power. As he issued his orders, he would often raise a hand to his cap and close his eyes in prayer. When asked later about his skill in manoeuvring *Carpathia* at high speed through the dangerous ice and bergs that lay ahead of his ship, he was quoted as saying: 'I can only conclude another hand than mine was on the helm.'

Meanwhile, the platitudes received by Rostron continued. *Titanic* survivors, including 'Unsinkable' Margaret (Molly) Brown, presented Rostron with a silver cup and gold medal for his efforts on the night of the sinking. The cup was sold at auction in October 2015 for $200,000. In addition to the Congressional Gold Medal, Rostron was also awarded the official thanks of Congress, the American Cross of Honor, a medal from the Liverpool Shipwreck and Humane Society, and a gold medal from the Shipwreck Society of New York.

Rostron would captain the *Carpathia* for another year before being promoted to larger liners in rapid succession, eventually becoming the Commodore of the entire Cunard fleet. He would retire in May 1931 but remained active in maritime activities, including leading the Southampton Master Mariners' Club. He would also pen his life's story, *Home from the Sea*. Nine years after his retirement, Rostron took ill and died of pneumonia on 4 November 1940. He was 71.

***

The *Carpathia*

Like *Titanic*, *Carpathia* would also meet her end at the bottom of the Atlantic. On 15 July 1918, she departed from Liverpool as part of a First World War convoy headed to Boston. Aboard were fifty-seven passengers and 166 crew members. In accordance with wartime procedures, the convoy travelled on a zig-zag course to avoid German submarines.

Shortly after 9.00 am, on the morning of 17 July, a torpedo was sighted approaching on her port side. The engines were ordered full astern and the helm was turned hard to starboard, but it was too late. *Carpathia* was struck near her No. 3 hatch by the torpedo fired by German submarine *U-55*. Shortly afterwards, another of the underwater missiles hit – this time, penetrating the engine room and killing three firemen and two trimmers. The damage disabled any ability to escape, as the engines were knocked out by the second impact. The damage also cut off power to *Carpathia*'s wireless set.

Left with little choice, Captain William Prothero used signal flags to notify other ships in the convoy as to her status and to ask for assistance. He then ordered rockets fired to attract the attention of nearby patrol boats. The remaining convoy steamed away at full speed to escape meeting the same fate.

Carpathia's bow soon began to sink and she developed a list to port. Captain William Prothero gave the order to abandon ship and all fifty-seven passengers and the surviving crew members boarded her eleven lifeboats. A total of 218 survived out of the 223 aboard.

Meanwhile, Captain Prothero, the chief officer, first and second officers and the gunners remained on the sinking ship, seeing to it that all the confidential books and documents were tossed into the sea. Finally, a lifeboat was summoned to come alongside, and they too left the ship as she continued to sink.

To ensure *Carpathia*'s doom, *U-55* surfaced and fired a third torpedo into the ship near the gunners' rooms, resulting in a massive explosion of the ammunition stored there. The sub then headed toward the lifeboats when the HMS *Snowdrop* arrived and drove away the submarine with gunfire. She then picked up the survivors to take them back to Liverpool.

For the beloved *Carpathia*, the end would come at 11.00 am at a position recorded by the *Snowdrop* as 49°25'N 10°25'W. She had lasted just 1 hour and 45 minutes after the torpedo strike before coming to rest about approximately 120 miles west of Fastnet in Ireland.

In the spring of 2000 – 82 years after her sinking – the wreck of the *Carpathia* was discovered near her last reported position, sitting upright on the seabed at a depth of 500 feet. Like *Titanic,* the salvage rights have been claimed by Premier Exhibitions Inc., which has brought up dozens of artefacts from the site. They first went on display in 2009 as a companion to the company's exhibition of items retrieved from the wreck of the *Titanic*.

***

The *Californian*

In the end, the *Californian* would meet the same fate as the *Carpathia* – being sunk by a German U-boat. In reality, two German U-Boats.

While the *Californian* remained in commercial service after the *Titanic* incident, she found herself under the control of the British government once the First World War broke out.

Early on 9 November 1915, she was en route from Salonica to Marseilles transporting equipment and troops in support of the Allies fighting the Battle of Gallipoli. Suddenly, she found herself torpedoed by German submarine *U-34*. She survived the initial attack and was taken under tow by a French patrol boat but was torpedoed again – this time by German submarine *U-35*. The second blast sealed her fate and she sank around 7.45 am in some 13,000 feet of water, approximately 60 miles south-south-west of Cape Matapan, Greece.

The *Californian*'s final resting place was less than 200 miles from where hospital ship HMHS *Britannic* – *Titanic*'s sister ship – would be sunk just over a year later by a German underwater mine.

***

The Lawsuits

A flurry of lawsuits was filed against the White Star Line by many survivors of the *Titanic* disaster, as well as by relatives of those who had died. In all, their claims totalled some $16 million.

White Star contested their claims, saying there was a contract clause within the passenger tickets which absolved the company of liability. Additionally, it stated that circumstances leading to the accident were unforeseeable.

Eventually, the plaintiffs and White Star settled for a total sum of only $664,000 on 17 December 1915. This amounted to roughly $300 for each of 2,224 passengers who had been aboard the ill-fated ship – not a substantial amount to be shared among all survivors and families of those killed in the disaster. In fact, the amount paid out came to less than 20 per cent of what survivors and families of *Titanic*'s deceased had demanded.

The $664,000 was distributed as follows:

- $500,000 – the amount distributed to American claimants.
- $50,000 – the amount distributed to British claimants.
- $114,000 – the amount used to pay interest and legal expenses related to the lawsuits.

As a result of the outcome, changes were made to liability laws to ensure that victims of such future disasters would be better compensated.

***

The *Titanic* Relief Fund

The families of *Titanic*'s crew fortunately fared a little bit better than the ship's passengers, thanks to a fund set up to assist them. Overall, public donations to the *Titanic* Relief Fund eventually totalled $2,133,900. Donations came from far and wide, including contributions from King George and Queen Mary.

In an effort to achieve fair compensation for those who would receive the aid, the administrators of the fund created a compensation plan that was based on the rank of each crew member and their wages. In all, seven classes of compensation were set up, providing weekly allowances ranging from $10 for the widows of officers, to $3.12 for widows of stewards. A provision was added that the annuities would end if a widow decided to remarry.

Of the amount raised, $700,000 would be set aside for the 1,461 dependants of the *Titanic*'s lost sailors, 592 of whom were children. The children's allowances would cease at the age of 16 for males and 18 for females.

Originally, there was some concern about the fund, as so-called relief funds were not always managed satisfactorily. But the trustees of the *Titanic* fund, acting under the supervision of the public trustee, a government official, and guided by great actuarial advice, were credited with developing a plan that would be properly used to benefit those affected by the disaster. Its greatest strength was that it would not be distributed all at once among those entitled to receive it, but gradually over a period of forty years. Those who reviewed the plan felt it would adequately care for and educate the children of the lost seamen, and help support their widows for the rest of their lives.

The *Titanic* Relief Fund was formally closed in 1959. A portion of the remaining balance it held was transferred into annuities, with the rest given to the Shipwrecked Fishermen and Mariners' Royal Benevolent Society.

***

SOLAS

As a direct result of the *Titanic* disaster, the International Convention for the Safety of Life at Sea (known as SOLAS) was first undertaken in 1914. This maritime treaty was designed to set minimum safety standards for the construction, equipment and operation of merchant ships. Nations which belong to the organisation ensure that ships flying their flags comply with these standards at a minimum.

In all, the SOLAS treaty outlines a range of requirements that ships must adhere to in order to operate in compliance with the treaty's provisions under their nation's flag. Many of its key provisions are a direct consequence of the deficiencies exposed by the loss of the *Titanic*. These include:

- The subdivision of passenger ships into watertight compartments so that after damage to its hull, a vessel will remain afloat and stable.
- Lifesaving appliances and arrangements for all passengers, including requirements for lifeboats, rescue boats and life jackets according to type of ship.
- Radio Communications Equipment. Today, this requires both passenger and cargo ships to carry approved radio equipment, including satellite Emergency Position Indicating Radio Beacons (EPIRBs) and Search and Rescue Transponders (SARTs).
- A requirement that governments ensure that all vessels are sufficiently and efficiently manned from a safety point of view. It places requirements on all vessels regarding voyage and passage planning, expecting a careful assessment of any proposed voyages by all who put to sea. Every mariner must take account of all potential dangers to navigation, weather forecasts, tidal predictions, the competence of the crew and all other relevant factors. It also adds an obligation for all vessels' masters to offer assistance to those in distress and controls the use of lifesaving signals with specific requirements regarding danger and distress messages. These apply to all vessels and their crews, including yachts and private craft, on all voyages and trips including local ones.
- Requires every ship owner and any person or company that has assumed responsibility for a ship to comply with the International

Safety Management Code. This includes an audit of shipping companies on a regular basis for proper operation and safety. After successful completion of an audit, a company is given a Document of Compliance, which is valid for five years.

- Confirms that the role of the Master in maintaining the security of the ship is not, and cannot be, constrained by the Company, the charterer or any other person.

Although the foundation for SOLAS began in 1914, its adoption was interrupted by the First World War. Further versions were adopted in 1929 and 1948. Since then, it has been regularly updated to reflect changes affecting shipping and the availability of new technologies.

SOLAS in its successive forms is generally regarded as the most important of all international treaties concerning the safety of merchant ships. Its development and implementation help to ensure that the 1,500 people who perished in the *Titanic* disaster did not die in vain.

Titanic: The 'What Ifs'

There were many circumstances that worked together to seal the fate of over 1,500 people who perished when *Titanic* slipped below the frigid North Atlantic in the early hours of 15 April 1912. Consider what might have been if any of these things had been different:

- What if the *Olympic* had not collided with the *Hawke* and delayed *Titanic*'s maiden voyage?
- What if the *Mesaba*'s warning about ice at 7.50 pm had carried the prefix 'MSG' so that it would have been required to go to *Titanic*'s captain, instead of being set aside in her wireless room?
- What if *Titanic*'s radio had not broken down and Phillips had not been so busy with a backlog of messages, allowing him to take Evans' final ice warning from the *Californian*?
- What if Officer Groves had known to wind up the detector on the *Californian*'s radio set so he could hear *Titanic*'s distress call?
- What if *Californian*'s captain or crew had responded to *Titanic*'s distress rockets?
- What if *Californian*'s radio operator had been awakened to find out what was going on?
- What if *Titanic* had held an emergency lifeboat drill so passengers and crew knew to which lifeboats they had been assigned?
- What if *Titanic*'s crew had been told the lifeboats were reinforced and could be fully loaded before launch without fear of buckling?
- What if *Titanic*'s lookouts had access to binoculars?
- What if the stronger steel originally specified for *Titanic*'s hull had been used?

- What if *Titanic*'s engines had not been reversed when the iceberg was spotted, perhaps allowing the ship to turn quicker and avoid the fatal collision?
- What if there had been moonlight so the lookouts could more easily spot the iceberg?
- What if the ocean had not been a dead calm and waves had been splashing against the iceberg, making it easier to see?
- What if *Titanic*'s original design plan had been followed, leaving forty-eight lifeboats in place?
- What if the bulkheads had been built as originally specified and made watertight all the way to the top of each compartment?
- What if White Star had done more to dispel the fallacy that *Titanic* was 'unsinkable'?

The 'what ifs' are almost endless. A difference in almost any one of these circumstances might have made *Titanic* just another footnote in the glory days of transatlantic travel.

Unfortunately, they all played a part in creating the most well-known maritime disaster in history.

Titanic: Timeline

- **1850:** The White Star Line – the company that will come to build and operate the *Titanic* – is founded.
- **1869:** Belfast shipbuilders Harland & Wolff start construction of ships for the White Star Line, beginning a long relationship between the two firms.
- **12 December 1862:** Bruce J. Ismay, future President of the White Star Line, is born in Crosby, England.
- **7 February 1873:** Thomas Andrews, future designer of the *Titanic*, is born in Comber, County Down, Ireland.
- **1891:** J. Bruce Ismay, the son of Thomas Henry, becomes a partner in the White Star Line. Following the death of his father, he will take over the role of chairman.
- **1894:** Lord William James Pirrie becomes the chairman of Harland & Wolff.
- **1898:** American author Morgan Robertson publishes a novel called '*Futility*' – a full 14 years before the *Titanic* tragedy. The book details the fate of a British ocean liner named *Titan*, which strikes an iceberg in April while on her maiden voyage in the North Atlantic. The ship sinks, resulting in the loss of her passengers and crew.
- **1902:** American financier J. Pierpont Morgan's shipping trust, the International Mercantile Marine Company (IMM), buys the White Star Line.
- **1904:** J. Bruce Ismay becomes President and Managing Director of International Mercantile Marine, and Harland & Wolff Chairman Lord William James Pirrie is named as one of IMM's Board of Directors.

- **7 April 1907:** Bruce and Florence Ismay have dinner with Lord Pirrie at his home in London. Pirrie and Ismay discuss creating a new fleet of transatlantic liners to compete with Cunard's new ships, the *Lusitania* and the *Mauretania*. Built with the help of a government subsidy, the Cunard ships have set new standards in luxurious ocean travel. To counter Cunard, Ismay and Pirrie decide to build the largest ships possible to maximise steerage capacity, White Star's main income source. However, they also decide to make the first- and second-class accommodations of their new ships the most luxurious possible in an effort to attract the wealthy and prosperous middle class as passengers. The first of these three great liners will eventually be named *Olympic* and the ships will be known as '*Olympic*-class.'

- **29 July 1908:** Thomas Andrews and other Harland & Wolff staff present blueprints and drawings for the proposed ships to Bruce Ismay and other White Star Line executives. Andrews has familiarised himself with every detail of the design to ensure the proposed ships meet every expectation. Andrews suggests the ships have forty-eight lifeboats (instead of twenty as it would have in the final design). He also proposes adding a double hull and watertight bulkheads that rise up to B deck – providing an additional margin of safety against sinking. He is overruled. Two days later, Ismay approves the design and signs three 'Letters of Agreement' authorising the start of construction. The cost of each liner is to be 'cost, plus' – an estimated $7,500,000, based on actual cost plus a 5% profit fee. At this point, the first ship, which will later be named *Olympic*, has no name. It is initially referred to simply as 'Number 400' – the 400th ship to be built by Harland & Wolff since its founding.

- **16 December 1908:** The keel for *Olympic* is first laid down at Harland & Wolff's shipyard in Belfast using newly built slipways especially designed for the construction of the new and massive *Olympic*-class liners.

- **31 March 1909:** *Titanic*'s keel is laid down in the slipway adjacent to *Olympic*.
- **20 October 1910:** *Olympic* is launched without fanfare or formal christening; the White Star Line traditionally never christens any of its vessels. For the launch, the hull is painted in a light grey colour so it photographs better in black and white pictures. This is the common practice for the first ship in a new class. *Olympic*'s hull is later repainted black after the launch, as black better hides the coal dust that stains the sides of liners when they are fuelled. The unfinished ship is then dry-docked for installation of boilers, engines, superstructure and funnels.
- **14 June 1911:** With her fitting-out complete, *Olympic* is placed into service on the transatlantic route.
- **31 May 1911:** *Titanic*'s unfinished hull is launched, again without a formal christening ceremony. 'They just builds em, and shoves em in!' declares a shipyard worker. Despite the lack of public ceremony, preparations for the launch of *Titanic* are very intricate. The weight of the hull needs to be transferred from the supports on which she was constructed to the launch way itself. This requires the careful removal of bilge blocks and keel blocks. The bow is held by a giant brace and 'dog shores' support the hull with wedges. Workers move along the length of the keel marking the various blocks with red, white and blue paint to indicate the order in which they are to be removed. The red blocks are removed the day before and early on the morning of 31 May, the white blocks are taken out. As the noon launch time approaches, the blue blocks located under her stern are removed as the tide comes in. The slipway is already coated with a mixture of 23 tons of tallow, train oil and soft soap, allowing the sliding ways beneath the hull of *Titanic* to ease down toward the water. At this point, the only things keeping the massive hull in place are the dog shores and a large launching trigger held under hydraulic pressure. At 12.05 pm,

signal rockets are fired and workers quickly knock out the dog shores. Next, a third rocket is fired at 12.10 pm to announce that *Titanic* is almost ready to launch. A few minutes later, Robert Keith, Head Foreman Shipwright at Harland & Wolff, activates a lever to drop the launching triggers. Moments later, he opens a second valve to allow the hydraulic rams to release the sliding ways on which *Titanic* is resting. At 12.13 pm, *Titanic* starts to move for the first time, amid the cheers of 100,000 spectators gathered to see the launch. The hull gathers speed estimated to be 12 knots (almost 14 miles per hour), and the great leviathan enters the water. *Titanic* is then taken to the fitting-out dock for installation of her superstructure, smokestacks, propellers and interior, including the electrical systems, wall coverings and furniture.

- **14 June 1911:** *Olympic*, having passed her sea trials, departs on her maiden voyage from Southampton to New York, with stops at Cherbourg, France, and Cobb, Ireland, where she will pick up additional passengers, mail and cargo.
- **30 November 1911:** The keel is laid down for *Britannic*, the third of the great liners in the *Olympic*-class.
- **31 March 1912:** Construction of *Titanic* is finished, 10 months after the launch of her hull. She is slightly different from her sister *Olympic*, with improvements based on experience from *Olympic*'s first year of service. Most noticeable of these is the forward half of *Titanic*'s A Deck promenade, which is enclosed by a steel screen with sliding windows. This is done to provide additional shelter from wind and waves, unlike *Olympic*'s promenade deck which is open along its entire length. This helps to increase *Titanic*'s gross weight to 46,328 tons, compared to *Olympic*'s 45,324 tons. As a result, *Titanic* is able to claim the title of being the largest ship in the world.
- **2 April 1912:** *Titanic* leaves Belfast for her sea trials, which includes tests of speed, turns and an emergency stop. Inspectors

sign off on her seaworthiness and approve her for passenger service. That evening, about 8.00 pm, *Titanic* heads to Southampton, England, to prepare for her maiden voyage to New York. An estimated crowd of 100,000 turns out along the shoreline to watch the ship leave, cheering, waving handkerchiefs and singing 'Rule Britannia!'.

- **3 April 1912:** *Titanic* arrives in Southampton dressed in flags and pennants. She is berthed in slip 44.
- **6 April 1912:** Crew hiring begins at the White Star Line offices and at union halls. Hundreds of people show up, hoping for a job after the national coal strike which has idled dozens of ships. Loading of cargo also begins, including the 5,800 tons of coal needed for the voyage.
- **7 April 1912:** Crews finish loading coal into *Titanic*'s bunkers and work stops for the day to observe Easter.
- **8 April 1912:** The *Titanic* continues to be loaded with supplies. Provisions include 75,000 pounds of fresh meat, 40 tons of potatoes, 40,000 eggs, 15,000 bottles of ale and 8000 cigars.
- **9 April 1912:** The British Board of Trade completes a final inspection of *Titanic* along with Captain E.J. Smith, Second Officer Charles Lightoller and builder Thomas Andrews. All of the ship's officers sleep aboard the ship except Captain Smith, who spends a last evening at home in Southampton with his family.
- **10 April 1912 – 7.30 am:** Captain Smith boards *Titanic* and receives the sailing report from Chief Henry Wilde. Bruce Ismay boards sometime after breakfast and tours the finished ship.
- **10 April 1912 – 9.30 am:** The first boat train arrives from Waterloo Station. From 9.30 am until 11.30 am, passengers board the ship.
- **10 April 1912 – 11.45 am:** *Titanic*'s mighty steam whistle sounds to signal her imminent departure. Crews prepare to withdraw the gangplanks.

- **10 April 1912 – 12.05 pm:** *Titanic*'s mooring ropes are released and tug boats begin towing her from her berth as she begins her maiden voyage.
- **10 April 1912 – 12.10 pm:** As *Titanic* moves from its dock and down the River Test, the suction from its passing hull snaps all six mooring lines of the *New York*, which is laid up nearby because of the national coal strike. The *New York* is pulled toward the *Titanic* and collision appears certain until *Titanic* adds power to its port propeller and uses the wash to push the *New York* away from it, narrowly avoiding disaster. Tugs quickly secure the *New York*, and *Titanic* proceeds on her ill-fated maiden voyage.
- **10 April 1912 – 6.30 pm:** First stop is in Cherbourg, France, where the *Titanic* arrives to load more passengers, mail and freight. She leaves at 8.10 pm, and heads to Queenstown, Ireland (now Cobh) – her final stop before heading across the North Atlantic.
- **11 April 1912 – 7.00 am:** Thomas Andrews and the nine member 'guarantee group' from Harland & Wolff hold a drill to test all of the ship's watertight safety doors.
- **11 April 1912 – 11.30 am:** *Titanic* arrives at Queenstown and anchors two miles off shore. White Star tenders *America* and *Ireland* deliver more passengers and mail.
- **11 April 1912 – 1.30 pm:** *Titanic* leaves Queenstown and begins her ill-fated journey across the Atlantic for New York. She is carrying an estimated 2,224 passengers and crew. This is less than her full capacity of 3,327 (2,435 passengers and 892 crew). She holds lifeboats with a capacity of only 1,178. Late this afternoon, she passes the Old Head of Kinsale and blows her whistles to acknowledge those on shore who have turned out to wave goodbye. She then heads out to the open sea.
- **12 April 1912:** At daybreak, *Titanic* is well on her way out to the North Atlantic. Sailing at 21 knots, she has covered 386 miles during her first day at sea. In the radio room, many

wireless messages are received offering congratulations on her maiden voyage. Some passengers prefer to stay inside the comforts of the warm ship as it is enveloped in very cold Atlantic winds.

- **13 April 1912:** The ship's wireless set has failed and operators Jack Phillips and Harold Bride spend hours troubleshooting the faulty set. Although Marconi Company rules require them to use a less powerful backup set, they eventually find a short circuit in the main set and fix it. It will turn out to be a crucial piece of luck when they need to send the call for assistance after the ship hits the iceberg just hours later.

- **13 April 1912 – 10.30 am:** Captain Smith starts his daily inspection of the ship. While checking the engine room he is told by Chief Engineer Bell that the coal bunker fire in boiler room 6 has finally been extinguished. However, the bulkhead bunker shows signs of heat damage. Smith orders oil to be rubbed on the damaged 1-inch-thick steel.

- **13 April 1912 – 12.00 pm:** *Titanic* has now covered 519 miles during the last 24 hours. Passengers continue to enjoy the pleasures and comforts of the luxurious ship. Steerage passengers find their accommodations on a par with second class on many other ships of the period. *Titanic*'s crew settles into its routine of running the ship and serving passengers.

- **14 April 1912 – 9.00 am:** Senior wireless operator Jack Phillips begins to receive warnings of icebergs from other vessels further to the west and ahead of *Titanic*. The first warning of the day comes from the liner *Caronia* which has spotted icebergs and growlers (small icebergs that are harder to see, but still dangerous) in 49 degrees to 51 degrees W. *Titanic* will cover another 546 miles this day before she comes upon the iceberg that will end her maiden voyage.

- **14 April 1912 – 10.15 am:** Captain Edward John Smith is given the first telegraph warning of icebergs lying ahead of his route.

- **14 April 1912 – 11.00 am:** The ship's first lifeboat drill is scheduled, but is cancelled by Captain Smith, who offers no explanation. The crew – most of whom are new to the ship – are left totally unprepared for the real lifeboat evacuation which will take place in just a few hours.

- **14 April 1912 – 12.00 pm:** Phillips receives the second ice warning of the day, from the steamship *Baltic*. The report relays that there are large icebergs in the area directly ahead of the *Titanic*.

- **14 April 1912 – 2.00 pm:** Captain Smith shows the second ice warning to Bruce Ismay, who places it in his pocket and shows it to other passengers later.

- **14 April 1912 – 5.30 pm:** Over the course of the next two hours, the air temperature drops from 10 degrees Celsius (51 Fahrenheit) to 1 degree Celsius (33 Fahrenheit).

- **14 April 1912 – 5.50 pm:** *Titanic* changes course from south-west to due west. This was originally planned to occur at 5.30 pm but is delayed to allow *Titanic* to travel further south in an attempt to avoid the ice region reported by the *Baltic*. This change should have moved *Titanic* into an area free of icebergs. This would have been the case in any normal year, but 1912 was not a normal year for ice. Cold water has pushed the warm gulfstream further south, and the change of course actually puts the ship in the direct path of the iceberg that will sink it.

- **14 April 1912 – 6.00 pm:** Second Officer Charles Lightoller takes over the bridge from Chief Officer Wilde.

- **14 April 1912 – 7.20 pm:** Assistant wireless operator Harold Bride finishes work on the accounts of passengers who will be charged for sending telegrams from the ship. He picks up the ice warning from the SS *Californian*, which states it has spotted three large icebergs at 42 degrees N, 49 degrees W. As Bride arrives on the bridge, he learns that Captain Smith has already left to dine with passengers. Bride later testifies during an inquiry that the telegram was passed to another officer instead. None of the surviving officers recall ever seeing the message.

- **14 April 1912 – 8.55pm:** Captain Smith checks in with the bridge before retiring to his cabin. The conditions this evening are moonless, clear and the sea is a flat calm. There is little wind and the calm waters make spotting an iceberg much more difficult as there will be no waves breaking against them. And, with little moonlight, there will be no reflections from any icebergs lying ahead.

- **14 April 1912 – 9.20 pm:** After dining with White Star President, Bruce Ismay, Captain Edward Smith visits the bridge to instruct that a sharp lookout be kept for ice. He remarks that the ship will have to slow down if there is any doubt about conditions, but he does not order any reduction in *Titanic*'s speed before retiring to his cabin.

- **14 April 1912 – 9.40 pm:** Senior radio operator Jack Phillips receives the fifth and final ice warning. It comes from the SS *Mesaba* and warns of a 'great number' of large icebergs and field ice just 15 miles ahead of the *Titanic* at latitude 42 degrees N to 41 degrees 25', longitude 49 degrees W. Because the message is not prefixed with 'MSG' – which would require the message to be given to the captain – Phillips treats it as being non-urgent. He fails to pass the message on to the bridge and returns to the task of sending the personal telegrams of passengers that had backed up while the transmitting equipment was broken and being fixed. Phillips is also likely distracted because there is only a two-hour window to send passenger telegrams via the Cape Race station on Newfoundland.

- **14 April 1912 – 10.00 pm:** Frederick Fleet and Reginald Lee begin their two-hour watch in the crow's nest. They have been instructed to look out for small growlers more than larger icebergs. Meanwhile, First Officer Murdoch takes over the bridge from Lightoller.

- **14 April 1912 – 10.55 pm:** The *Californian* breaks into Phillips' transmissions to send a message informing the *Titanic* that she has stopped sailing for the night because she has come upon a large field of ice. The ice lies just a short distance ahead of the *Titanic*, but Phillips harshly replies with 'Shut up! Shut up! I am busy. I am working Cape Race.' Meanwhile, unbeknown to Murdoch, the fatal iceberg now lies just 15 miles ahead. *Titanic* continues at 21.5 knots (24 miles per hour), nearly her top speed.

- **14 April 1912 – 11.00 pm:** Most of the *Titanic*'s passengers have retired to their rooms for the evening. A few men remain in the smoking lounge as stewards prepare the dining areas for the morning's breakfast.

- **14 April 1912 – 11.30 pm:** Lookouts Fleet and Lee note a slight haze appearing ahead. *Titanic* is moving near her top speed and is covering almost 2200 feet per minute. The iceberg now lies just 4 miles ahead. *Titanic* will reach it in less than 10 minutes. Meanwhile, the *Californian*'s radio operator, Cyril Evans, shuts down his wireless set and turns in for the night. The ship closest to the *Titanic* has now gone deaf for the night.

- **14 April 1912 – 11.39 pm:** The iceberg is only 1,000 yards ahead now, but the moonless conditions and calm sea mean the lookouts have still not spotted it. As he squints into the darkness, lookout Frederick Fleet suddenly sees a massive shape looming out of the night. He rings the crow's nest bell three times to indicate that something is ahead and then grabs the telephone and calls the bridge. He is asked 'What have you seen?' – to which he yells back: 'Iceberg, right ahead!' But his warning will come too late.

- **14 April 1912 – 11.40 pm:** Alerted by the crow's nest, Murdoch orders the ship's wheel be put hard over to starboard to steer away from the berg. He also orders the engines put into reverse, unwittingly making the rudder less effective in turning the ship. Precious seconds pass before the bow begins to turn, but it is not enough and *Titanic* hits the iceberg, striking the starboard side. Despite the collision, many passengers and crew sleep through it and many others – including lookout Fleet – assume the ship has survived a glancing blow and is undamaged.

- **14 April 1912 – 11.43 pm:** Captain Smith enters the bridge and is quickly told what has happened. He instructs the ship's engineer to sound the vessel for damage and report back.
- **14 April 1912 – 11.55 pm:** Smith is given the news – the ship appears badly damaged and is taking water fast in five compartments. *Titanic*'s designer Thomas Andrews – aboard the maiden voyage to note any problems – knows the ship can float with the first four compartments flooded, but not five. He quickly calculates that *Titanic* cannot overcome the damage and will only stay afloat one or two hours longer – perhaps a little more depending on the pumps.
- **14 April 1912 – 12.00 am:** Lookouts Frederick Fleet and Reginald Lee are relieved from the crow's nest and proceed to the boat deck where they will shortly be ordered to prepare the lifeboats.
- **15 April 1912 – 12.15 am:** Captain Smith enters the radio room and orders that an emergency request for assistance be broadcast to all ships within range. Cape Race hears *Titanic*'s CQD giving her position as 41.44 N., 50.24 W. Other ships receiving the initial distress message include the *La Provence* and the *Mount Temple*. But the nearest ship, the *Californian*, will not hear the distress call, as she has turned off her wireless set for the evening after receiving Phillips' curt response just an hour before. Although just a few miles away, her help will never come.
- **15 April 1912 – 12.15 am:** *Ypiranga* hears C.Q.D. from *Titanic*. *Titanic* gives C.Q.D. 'Position 41.44 N., 50.24 W. Require assistance' (calls about 10 times).
- **15 April 1912 – 12.20 am:** Fully realising that his ship has little time left, Captain Smith orders his officers to start loading the

lifeboats. Smith orders women and children first – but his order is taken differently by the officers. Some believe Smith has ordered women and children *only*, while other officers believe he means women and children first, then men if there is room left in a lifeboat.

- **15 April 1912 – 12.25 am:** Although SOS had become the official distress signal, many radio operators still use CQD – 'CQ' signifying 'calling any station' and 'D' meaning distress. During the next 100 minutes, Phillips sends out both. The *Frankfurt* is among the first to respond, but the liner is some 170 nautical miles away to the south. Other ships also offer assistance – including *Titanic*'s sister ship, the *Olympic* – but all are too far away to help in time. *Carpathia*'s radio operator, who has also heard *Titanic*'s distress call, replies that he has informed his captain and that his ship has put about and is heading for the *Titanic* with all possible speed. *Carpathia* is 58 miles away – and it will take an estimated 4 hours to cover the distance. Phillips urges they hurry at all possible speed: 'Come at once. We have struck a berg. It's a C.Q.D. O.M. Position 41.46 N. 50.14 W.'
- **15 April 1912 – 12.36 am:** The *Prinz Friedrich Wilhelm* calls M.G.Y. (*Titanic*) and gives position at 12.00 am as 39.47 N., 50.10 W. *Titanic* says, 'Are you coming to our...?' *Frankfurt* says: 'What is the matter with u?'. *Titanic* desperately replies: 'We have collision with iceberg. Sinking. Please tell Captain to come.' *Frankfurt* replies: 'O.K, will tell.'
- **15 April 1912 – 12.45 am:** Lifeboat 7 on the starboard side is first to be launched under the direction of Officers Murdoch and Lowe. The boat leaves with just twenty-eight people on board, far less than its capacity of sixty-five. Meanwhile, Captain Smith and other crew members believe they see a ship in the distance. It is likely the *Californian* – and Smith gives the order to begin sending up distress rockets. The first of eight emergency distress rockets is fired. There is no response from the other ship.

- **15 April 1912 – 12.50 am:** Officers standing watch on the *Californian* discuss the rockets they have seen being fired by another ship. They call up their captain, Stanley Lord, who has retired to his cabin. They tell Lord what they have been watching and he is asked if they are 'company signals'. After a brief conversation, Lord says to keep him informed, but goes back to sleep. Eventually the officers on deck call Lord again to say the ship has turned and sailed away. But this is likely just an illusion. As the *Titanic*'s brightly-lit portholes slipped under the water, it was only giving the impression of turning away to those watching from a distance.

- **15 April 1912 – 1.00 am:** Bandleader Wallace Hartley seeks to calm *Titanic*'s passengers by having his musicians play music during the sinking. They will play almost until the end. Their last song remains somewhat of a mystery, with many claiming it was 'Nearer My God to Thee'. However, Marconi operator Harold Bride would dispute this, telling *The New York Times* it was a song named 'Songe d'Automne' (Autumn).

- **15 April 1912 – 1.10 am:** Lifeboat 6 is ordered to be lowered away although it only has twenty-nine of its sixty-five seats filled. Lookout Frederick Fleet is ordered into the boat by Second Officer Charles Lightoller and he takes a position at the oars. Also aboard is 'Unsinkable' Molly Brown, who calls out that another oarsman is needed. Major Arthur Godfrey Peuchen of the Royal Canadian Yacht Club volunteers to help and shimmies down the ropes into the boat. Peuchen is the only adult male passenger Lightoller permits to board a lifeboat.

- **15 April 1912 – 1.20 am:** Lifeboat 10 is launched from the port side with forty-seven people. Thomas Andrews is seen staring at a painting in the first-class smoking room and is told he should try to save himself. Andrews does not reply.

- **15 April 1912 – 1.25 am:** Panic is now setting in as lifeboat 14 is launched from the starboard side with fifty-four people, including Officer Lowe. Lowe fires three shots in the air from his pistol to keep passengers on the lower deck from jumping onto the boat. About the same time, lifeboat 16 is launched from the port side with forty-two people. Meanwhile, *Olympic* sends its position to *Titanic* as 40.52 N., 61.18 W. 'Are you steering southerly to meet us?' *Titanic* replies: 'We are putting the women off in the boats.'

- **15 April 1912 – 1.35 am:** *Baltic* hears *Titanic* say 'Engine room getting flooded.'
- **15 April 1912 – 1.40 am:** Cape Race says to *Virginian*: 'Please tell your captain this: The *Olympic* is making all speed for *Titanic* but his [*Olympic's*] position is 40.32 N., 61.18 W. You are much nearer *Titanic*. The *Titanic* is already putting women off in the boats, and he says the weather there is calm and clear.' The *Olympic* is the only ship we have heard say, 'Going to the assistance of the *Titanic.*' The others must be a long way from the *Titanic.*'
- **15 April 1912 – 1.45 am:** Last signals heard from *Titanic* by *Carpathia*, 'Engine room full up to boilers.'
- **15 April 1912 – 1.47 am:** *Caronia* hears M.G.Y. (*Titanic*) though the signals are unreadable.
- **15 April 1912 – 1.48 am:** *Asian* hears *Titanic* call '*S.O.S.*' *Asian* answers *Titanic* but receives no answer.
- **15 April 1912 – 1.50 am:** *Caronia* hears *Frankfurt* calling *Titanic*. *Frankfurt* is 172 miles from *Titanic* at the time the first 'S.O.S.' is sent out.
- **15 April 1912 – 1.55 am:** Cape Race says to *Virginian* 'we have not heard Titanic for about half an hour. His power may be gone.'
- **15 April 1912 – 2.00 am:** *Virginian* hears *Titanic* calling very faintly, her power being greatly reduced.
- **15 April 1912 – 2.10 am:** *Virginian* faintly hears the letter 'V' sent twice in Morse Code in a spark style similar to *Titanic's*. The *Virginian's* radio operator figures the *Titanic* is probably

adjusting its spark transmitter. Meanwhile, collapsible lifeboat D on the port side is the last to be successfully launched. Passengers are now jumping from the aft steerage loading door to the freezing water 100 feet below. *Titanic*'s propellers are now completely out of the water. Father Thomas Byles gives confession to passengers gathered on the aft end of the boat deck as loud and horrible crashes rock the ship. As the hull tilts ever higher, boilers and machinery in the bowels of the ship slam toward the submerged bow.

- **15 April 1912 – 2.17 am:** Phillips sends a final distress signal. *Virginian* hears *Titanic* call 'C.Q.', but is unable to read the blurred and ragged signals that follow. *Titanic*'s signals end very abruptly as though its power is suddenly cut off. The *Virginian* calls M.G.Y. (*Titanic*) and suggests he should try the ship's emergency set, but hears no response. Phillips finally leaves his post and makes it to the overturned collapsible lifeboat B but eventually succumbs to exposure and dies. His body is never found.

- **15 April 1912 – 2.18 am:** Collapsible lifeboat B floats off the port side as the ship goes under, but its launch is unsuccessful as there is not enough time to pull its canvas sides in place. At the same time, the *Titanic*'s lights go out, plunging the ship into total darkness.

- **15 April 1912 – 2.20 am:** *Titanic*'s bow sinks further and the stern rises higher out of the water. The incredible forces place a massive strain on the midsection until the ship breaks in two between the third and fourth funnels. Research later speculates it took about 6 minutes for the bow section to reach the ocean bottom at a depth of 12,415 feet. When it hits, it is estimated to be travelling at an estimated 30 miles per hour. After the bow snaps off, the stern momentarily settles back in the water before rising again, becoming almost vertical. It briefly remains in that position before it too slips beneath the surface. The once mighty liner has left hundreds of passengers and crew behind. The temperature of the ocean water is close to freezing as they struggle to stay afloat amid the quick onset of deadly hypothermia. They plea for help, but the lifeboats stay out of reach, their occupants afraid of being swamped if they return. Within 15 minutes, those in the water have become disoriented, exhausted and soon unconscious. The heartiest survive perhaps 45 minutes to an hour before death finally sets in.

- **15 April 1912 – 2.24 am:** The stern section implodes 200 feet below the surface due to external pressure, which releases the air still trapped inside. A huge bubble of roiling water bursts from the surface where the stern has gone down.

- **15 April 1912 – 2.31 am:** About this time, the stern hits the bottom landing some 2000 feet away from the bow at 41°43'35'N, 49°56'54'W.

- **15 April 1912 – 3.00 am:** Officers and crew begin to gather the scattered lifeboats together. Officer Lowe transfers some of his passengers to other boats and then heads for the people in the water to look for other survivors. Six people are pulled from the water, but they are barely alive. Another fourteen are pulled from the partially submerged collapsible A, which is then cast adrift with three dead bodies aboard. Lifeboats 4 and 12 take aboard twenty-eight survivors from overturned collapsible B.

- **15 April 1912 – 3.30 am:** The first of *Carpathia's* rockets are spotted as it races to the scene of the disaster. Survivors in the lifeboats begin setting paper and clothing on fire, hoping to be seen by the rescue ship.

- **15 April 1912 – 4.10 am:** *Carpathia* arrives and starts to bring survivors of the *Titanic* on board from the lifeboats. Lifeboat 2 is the first to be rescued. It will take several hours for the ship to pick up all 705 survivors.

- **15 April 1912 – 5.30 am:** The *Californian's* radio operator wakes up and turns on his set to finally be alerted to the *Titanic* disaster by the *Frankfurt*. Captain Lord is immediately informed and he orders his ship to steam to the scene of the sinking.

- **15 April 1912 – 7.15 am:** *Baltic,* after a wireless exchange with *Carpathia*, turns round for Liverpool, having steamed 134 miles west towards *Titanic*.
- **15 April 1912 – 8.30 am:** The last of the lifeboats (No.12) is rescued by the *Carpathia*. Officer Lightoller is the last survivor to come aboard. Meanwhile, the *Californian* has arrived and also combs the disaster area looking for survivors. It finds none.
- **15 April 1912 – 8.50 am:** Following a brief prayer service in the first-class dining room, *Carpathia* sets sail for New York, with 705 survivors aboard. An estimated 1,522 of *Titanic's* passengers and crew are believed lost at sea. White Star President Bruce Ismay, who entered a lifeboat at the last minute, sends a telegram from the *Carpathia* to the White Star Line's New York office: 'Deeply regret advise you Titanic sank this morning fifteenth after collision iceberg, resulting serious loss life; further particulars later.' Meanwhile, Captain Arthur Rostron of the *Carpathia* orders the ship's radio operator not to respond to the many inquiries being received from newspapers and others asking for details about the tragedy.
- **18 April 1912 – 9.25 pm:** The *Carpathia* arrives in New York in a cold rain, first visiting Pier 59 to deliver the *Titanic's* empty lifeboats back into the hands of White Star Line. It then moves on to Pier 54, where *Carpathia's* own passengers and the *Titanic* survivors disembark. They are greeted by massive crowds. Radio operator Harold Bride is met by both Guglielmo Marconi and *The New York Times*, which gives him $1,000 and publishes 'Thrilling Story by Titanic's Surviving Wireless Man'. Bride will return to the sea for a few years, but leave it for good in 1922 when he marries and takes a job as a salesman.
- **19 April 1912:** The United State Senate opens an investigation in New York into the sinking of the *Titanic*, the same day the

Californian quietly arrives in Boston. The hearing is chaired by Senator William Alden Smith and the first witness is White Star Chairman, J. Bruce Ismay. Then, on 22 April, the inquiry discovers that a ship near *Titanic* had failed to respond to the distress signals. The identity of the ship is unknown.

- **20 April 1912 – 6.00 am:** The cable repair ship *Mackay-Bennett* arrives at the site of the sinking to recover bodies after being contracted by the White Star Line. Among those on board are Canon Kenneth Cameron Hind of All Saints Cathedral, Halifax and John R. Snow, Jr., the chief embalmer with the firm of John Snow & Co., Nova Scotia's largest undertaking firm. The ship also carries embalming supplies to handle seventy bodies, 100 coffins and 100 tons of ice to preserve the recovered bodies. The body of first-class passenger John Jacob Astor IV, the richest man aboard *Titanic*, is embalmed and placed in a coffin, as is the body of Isador Straus, the owner of Macy's. Second-class passengers who are recovered are embalmed and wrapped in burlap. A total of 116 third-class passengers are buried at sea. After a week-long recovery mission, *Mackay-Bennett* returns with 190 corpses. Some 100 of the victims will be buried in the *Titanic* section of the Fairview Cemetery in Halifax. Hundreds of other victims are never recovered.

- **22 April 1912:** The Senate inquiry discovers that a ship near *Titanic* had failed to respond to the distress signals. The identity of the ship is unknown.

- **23 April 1912:** *The Clinton Daily Item*, a small New England newspaper, prints a shocking story claiming that *Californian* had refused aid to *Titanic*. The source of the story is *Californian*'s carpenter, James McGregor, who states that his ship had been close enough to see *Titanic*'s lights and distress rockets. On the same day, the *Boston American* newspaper carries a similar story by *Californian*'s assistant engineer, Ernest Gill. Gill and the *Californian*'s Captain, Stanley Lord, are subpoenaed to testify at the Senate hearing, where Gill repeats his story. Meanwhile, Lord gives conflicting testimony but admits he was aware of rockets being seen. However, he claims to believe they were 'company signals' – not distress rockets. Like the British Inquiry that will follow, the U.S. Senate committee concludes Lord failed to come to the aid of the sinking *Titanic*.

- **24 April 1912:** Just before *Olympic*'s next scheduled sailing for New York, 284 of the ship's firemen start a mutiny, refusing to sail on the ship citing an inadequate number of lifeboats and the safety of the forty second-hand collapsible boats that have been hastily added on board. In all, fifty-four firemen are formally charged with mutiny. On 4 May, British magistrates find the charges of mutiny proven, but discharge them without jail sentences or fines because of the special circumstances of the case. Fearing the public will side with the workers, the White Star Line rehires them and *Olympic* finally sails for New York on 15 May.

- **30 April 1912:** Jock Hume was a violinist aboard the *Titanic* who perished with the rest of the ship's band in the sinking. His father, Andrew, receives a bill for his son's band uniform from the agency that booked the musicians: 'Dear Sir: We shall be obliged if you will remit us the sum of 5s. 4d., which is owing to us as per enclosed statement. We shall also be obliged if you will settle the enclosed uniform account. Yours faithfully, C.W. & F.N. Black.' The uniform account included items such as: lyre lapel insignia (2 shillings), and sewing White Star buttons on tunic (1 shilling).' Andrew Hume decides not to settle the bill.

- **May 1912:** The first film about the sinking is released. *Saved from the Titanic* stars 22-year-old Dorothy Gibson, a popular actress who was actually on board when the ship sank. Gibson has an existing contract with the French film company Éclair and sees an opportunity to profit off the tragedy. Almost immediately after the wreck, she works to co-write the film, which will also be a starring vehicle for her.

- **2 May 1912:** In London, the British Board of Trade opens its inquiry into the sinking of *Titanic,* overseen by High Court judge Lord Mersey. It continues until 3 July 1912 with testimony from over 100 witnesses. Its findings mostly mirror those of the American investigation, blaming the ship's excessive speed, lack of sufficient lifeboats, and an unprepared crew. But it also finds the *Californian* at fault for not attempting rescue efforts. However, it does not lay blame on Captain Smith, noting he was following standard practice at the time of the wreck. In addition. Lord Mersey's final report does not blame the Board of Trade's insufficient regulations, including its outdated rules which do not require lifeboats for all on board. The report is generally well received. But *Titanic*'s surviving Second Officer, Charles Lightoller, considers it a whitewash and says: 'Apart from protecting itself, the [Board of Trade] had no interest in seeing the White Star Line found negligent. Any damage to White Star's reputation or balance sheet would be bad for British shipping – and there was considerable potential for both.'

- **3 July 1912:** After public hearings lasting thirty-six days, the U.S. Senate committee investigation finds that the *Titanic* was lost due to travelling at excessive speed in a region of known ice hazards. However, neither Captain Smith nor the ship's crew is judged to be at fault as this was standard practice at the time. In its findings, the panel calls for all ships to carry lifeboats with capacity for all passengers and crew. Previously, the outdated lifeboat regulations have been based on a ship's total tonnage, not the number of passengers.

- **August 1912:** The Leyland Line fires *Californian* Captain Stanley Lord. Lord eventually gets work with another shipping line and spends the rest of his life seeking to clear his name.

- **30 January 1914:** In response to the sinking of the *Titanic*, the International Conference on the Safety of Life at Sea (SOLAS) approves the establishment of the service which will become the International Ice Patrol. However, immediately following the sinking of *Titanic* in April 1912, the U.S. Navy had begun patrolling the outer banks of Newfoundland using the cruisers USS *Chester* and USS *Birmingham*. Since the International Ice Patrol was established, it has been operated by the U.S. Coast Guard, but funded by the many countries that were signatories to SOLAS. The Marconi Company has also implemented a new rule – it now requires every ship carrying its equipment to maintain radio operations for 24 hours a day.

- **26 February 1914:** *Britannic* is launched with many new safety features learned from the *Titanic* disaster, including a double hull. Because of the outbreak of the First World War, she is laid up for months at Harland & Wolff in Belfast before being requisitioned by the British government as a hospital ship. Work is completed on 12 December 1915 and she enters service to return sick and wounded soldiers from Greece.

- **9 November 1915:** The *Californian*, now serving as a First World War cargo vessel under British control, is torpedoed during the early hours by German submarine *U-34* about 61 miles south-west of Cape Matapan, Greece. While under tow, she is torpedoed again by *U-35* and sinks around 7.45 am. One crewman is killed and three are injured.

- **17 December 1915:** *Titanic*'s owner, Oceanic Steam Navigation Company, reaches a settlement with claimants and pays a total of $664,000 to be shared among the victims of the sinking and their families. Claims had originally totalled some $16,000,000.

- **6 June 1916:** *Britannic* returns to Belfast to undergo the necessary modifications for transforming her into a transatlantic passenger liner. The British government pays the White Star Line £75,000 to compensate for the conversion. The transformation is under way until it is interrupted by a recall of the ship back into military service on 26 August 1916.

- **21 November 1916 – 8.12 am**: *Britannic* hits a German mine while sailing near the Greek island of Kea. She sinks in just 55 minutes, killing thirty people. In all, 1,065 people are on board, with 1,035 survivors rescued from the water and from lifeboats. *Britannic* was the largest ship lost in the First World War.
- **17 July 1918 – 9.15 am:** While sailing as the lead ship in a First World War convoy, the *Carpathia* is torpedoed three times and sunk by German submarine *U-55* south-east of Ireland and west of the Isles of Scilly. Of the 223 aboard, 218 survive.
- **1922:** White Star obtains three German ocean liners given to Britain as war reparations under the terms of the Treaty of Versailles. These were to replace the *Britannic*, *Oceanic*, *Arabic*, *Cymric* and *Laurentic*, all of which had been lost in the First World War. These ships were the former SS *Bismarck* – which was renamed *Majestic*; the SS *Berlin* – renamed *Arabic*; and the SS *Columbus* – renamed *Homeric*. The *Majestic* was then the world's largest liner at 56,551 gross tons, becoming the company's flagship. The former German liners operate successfully alongside *Olympic* until the Great Depression reduces passenger demand.
- **1923:** White Star and Cunard reach an agreement to alternate their departures during the winter months, allowing them to use fewer ships during this less profitable season. It also permits ships that are out of service to be overhauled and refitted.
- **1 January 1927:** Lord Kylsant, now head of Harland & Wolff since the death of Lord Pirrie in 1924, buys back all the shares in the White Star Line for £7,907,661. The move makes Kylsant the owner of the largest fleet of ships in the world, as he also owns the Royal Mail Steam Packet Company (RMSPC).
- **1928:** White Star orders a new liner to be called *Oceanic*, the same name as an earlier ship in the company's fleet. The keel of the 1,000-foot vessel is laid down at Harland & Wolff, but is stopped the following year as the Great Depression hits. Work on

the ship never resumes and her keel is eventually dismantled with the steel used for other ships.

- **1929:** Facing a drop in passenger bookings and lost revenue, White Star begins limiting its expenditures and sells off several of its older ships. Many transatlantic crossings are cancelled as well. *Olympic* and *Majestic* are also used as cruise ships in an effort to bring in more money.

- **1930:** A new *Britannic* enters passenger service for White Star and she makes a profit due to her modern and economical design. She is used for transatlantic service, as well as for cruises. However, it is not enough and White Star posts its first deficit ever.

- **1931:** Lord Kylsant departs White Star, leaving the company on the verge of bankruptcy. Former Chairman Bruce Ismay returns after a twenty-year hiatus in an attempt to save the company from being dissolved. He tries to enlist the aid of the British government, but his plan fails to materialise. With the company heavily indebted to banks, the financial institutions begin playing a major role in White Star's operations.

- **10 May 1934:** With both companies facing financial problems because of the Great Depression, the British government agrees to financially back White Star and Cunard, but only on the condition that they merge. Cunard-White Star Limited is formed as a result. In 1949, Cunard will drop the White Star reference from the company's name.

- **5 April 1935:** *Olympic* is retired. During her lifetime in commercial service, she has completed 257 round trips across the Atlantic, carried some 430,000 passengers and travelled 1,800,000 miles – earning her the nickname 'Old Reliable.' Cunard-White Star briefly considers using *Olympic* for summer cruises. This proposal is dropped and she is put up for sale. Potential buyers include a syndicate that proposes using her as a floating hotel off the south coast of France. This idea is also abandoned.

- **11 October 1935**: *Olympic* leaves Southampton for the final time and sails to Jarrow for initial demolition. Between 1935 and 1937, her superstructure is demolished. In September 1937, *Olympic*'s hull is towed to Inverkeithing for final demolition, which is completed by late 1937.

- **17 October 1937:** Former White Star Chairman J. Bruce Ismay suffers a stroke and dies at the age of 74. His death follows years of depression, guilt and self-isolation because of the *Titanic* tragedy and his survival of the sinking, for which he has been vilified.

- **4 November 1940:** Retired *Carpathia* Captain Arthur Rostron dies of pneumonia at the age of 71 in Chippenham, Wiltshire, England.

- **8 December 1952**: Charles Lightoller, former Second Officer on the *Titanic* and the most senior officer to survive the sinking, dies at the age of 78. Following the *Titanic* disaster, he returned to sea and served in the Royal Navy. In June 1918, he commanded the warship HMS *Garry* to ram German submarine *UB-110*. In 1940, and while in retirement, Lightoller crossed the English Channel in his private motor yacht *Sundowner* to rescue 127 British soldiers who were pinned down at Dunkirk by German forces.

- **November 1955:** Walter Lord publishes *A Night to Remember*, the first book to accurately detail the events surrounding the loss of the *Titanic*. Lord wrote the book after tracking down and interviewing sixty-three survivors of the wreck, developing a minute-by-minute account of the events surrounding the disaster.

- **29 April 1956:** Harold Bride, the *Titanic*'s junior radio operator, dies from cancer at the age of 66 in Glasgow, Scotland.

- **3 July 1958:** Walter Lord's book, *A Night to Remember* is released as a film. It tells the story of the *Titanic*'s sinking in 123 minutes. Although the film is considered the definitive cinematic telling of the story, its box-office results are disappointing. The following year, it earns the Samuel Goldwyn International Award for the UK at the Golden Globe Awards.

- **24 January 1962:** Former *Californian* Captain Stanley Lord dies aged 84 in Wallasey, Cheshire, England. His son, Stanley Tutton Lord, continues the fight to clear his father's name until his own death in 1994.

- **10 January 1965**: *Titanic* lookout Frederick Fleet commits suicide, hanging himself at the age of 77. He had served as a lookout on the *Olympic* first, then on *Titanic*. He returned to those duties on the *Olympic* but left when he found former members of the *Titanic* were often treated with disdain. In later years, he became financially despondent and depressed. He ends his life a few months after his wife passes away and her brother evicts him from his home where he had been staying.

- **1981:** The year Douglas Woolley of East London, a retired pensioner, claims he filed salvage and ownership rights to the wreck of the *Titanic*. Having once worked in a nylon factory, he says he plans to use the material (because he says it floats) to raise the ship off the seabed. Woolley also claims to own the salvage rights to RMS *Queen Elizabeth*, which sank in Hong Kong harbour in 1972 after it caught fire. In 1974, Woolley planned to raise it first as a test, but gave up after investors pulled out. In January 2011, Woolley posts a message on LinkedIn still seeking investors. His new plan is to tow the *Titanic* underwater to Scotland, rustproof its remains and raise them. He then plans to weld it to the salvaged Queen Elizabeth and bring it to Liverpool as a tourist attraction. Years pass, but his dream remains unrealised.

- **1 September 1985:** A joint French-American expedition led by Jean-Louis Michel and Robert Ballard discovers the wreck of the *Titanic* in the North Atlantic at position 41°43'32"N 49°56'49"W, approximately 370 miles south-south-east of Newfoundland. This is about 13.7 miles from the position it gave during the distress calls it sent in 1912.

- **12 July 1986:** During a second season of exploring the site, Ballard dives to the wreck in a submersible. He places a plaque on *Titanic*, urging that the site be left undisturbed as a memorial. Congress passes the RMS Titanic Maritime Memorial Act, which directs the United States to enter into negotiations with other interested nations to establish guidelines to protect the 'scientific, cultural, and historical significance of RMS Titanic.' The Department of State contacts the United Kingdom, France, and Canada but finds they have little interest in such an agreement.

- **July 1987:** Titanic Ventures, a limited partnership, becomes salvor-in-possession of the wreck and begins to salvage artefacts from the site. The company contracts with the French organisation IFREMER, which makes thirty-two dives to the site and recovers some 1,800 artefacts. The operation draws strong protests and one *Titanic* survivor, Eva Hart, criticises the 'insensitivity and greed' and labels the operators of the salvage operation 'fortune hunters, vultures, pirates.' Facing financial difficulties, Titanic Ventures later sells its salvage interests and artefacts to RMS *Titanic*, Inc. (RMST). The company operates exhibits that display the many items brought up from the wreck, including the *Titanic*'s massive steam-powered whistles.

- **10 May 1996**: The U.S. District Court for the Eastern District of Virginia rejects a suit seeking to remove RMS *Titanic* as salvor-in-possession of the wreck.

- **1 November 1997:** The film *Titanic* is first released in Tokyo, followed by the American premiere the following month. It presents the love story of two fictional passengers – Jack of third class and Rose of first class – which is grafted on to the actual tragedy. Produced at a budget of $200 million, it includes actual footage of the wreck on the bottom of the North Atlantic, as well as detailed recreations of the ship during her maiden voyage. The film returns a box office of over $1.2 billion worldwide, and wins four Golden Globes and eleven Academy Awards. Oddly, director James Cameron has shot scenes involving the *California*'s radio warnings to the *Titanic* about the ice lying just ahead of her, but he chooses to leave them out of the final release of the film. Many *Titanic* historians believe the decision omits a critical piece of the tragedy, diminishing the film's value in telling the real story.

- **1998:** Deep Ocean Expeditions advertises its 'Operation Titanic.' It offers individuals the chance to visit the wreck in a Russian submersible for $32,500. RMST requests a preliminary injunction, and, in an order dated 23 June, the court declares that RMST, as salvor-in-possession, has the right to exclude others from visiting the site in order to photograph it. Despite the court injunction, 'Operation Titanic' visits the wreck site in September.

- **February 1999:** For the first time in 87 years, *Titanic*'s massive whistles – which have been recovered from the wreck's forward funnel – are heard again by the public during a demonstration at Union Depot in St. Paul, Minnesota. The 750-pound set of three whistles had first been brought to Kahlenberg Brothers Co. in Two Rivers, Wisconsin, for testing by the company which manufactures marine sound signals. After X-rays, a thorough cleaning and structural testing, the whistles are sounded using compressed air, as there is concern using steam might damage them.

- **24 March 1999:** A Federal Circuit court reverses the earlier ruling, stating that RMST cannot exclude others from visiting, viewing or photographing the *Titanic* site. RMST appeals to the Supreme Court but, in October, the High Court declines to review the case, leaving the company without exclusive photographic rights.

- **28 July 2001:** New Yorkers David Leibowitz and Kimberley Miller are married while aboard a submersible that has landed on the bow of the *Titanic*. Leibowitz had won a contest sponsored by a company that sells rides to the wreck site for $36,000 each. Asked if his girlfriend could come with him and he is told 'yes' – if they get married while visiting the wreck. The stunt is harshly criticised by relatives of the *Titanic*'s victims.

- **31 May 2009:** Eliza Gladys 'Millvina' Dean, the last survivor of the sinking of RMS *Titanic*, dies at the age of 97. At two months old, she is the youngest passenger aboard on the ship's maiden – and final – voyage. Her death comes exactly 98 years after *Titanic* was launched in Belfast.
- **2010:** For the first time, researchers begin mapping the entire wreck site of the *Titanic* on the ocean floor. They hope the comprehensive record of the entire 3-by-5-mile *Titanic* debris field will provide new clues about what exactly happened in 1912.
- **5 April 2012:** A century after her sinking, the wreck of the *Titanic* is to come under the protection of the United Nations cultural agency, UNESCO. The organisation declares the remains of the ship will fall under the 2001 Convention on the Protection of Underwater Cultural Heritage once it passes the 100th anniversary of its sinking on 15 April 2012.
- **April 2012:** Australian billionaire Clive Palmer announces he will build *Titanic II*, a replica of the original ill-fated liner. Palmer plans to make it the flagship of his proposed cruise company, Blue Star Line. While *Titanic* was 46,000 gross tons, Palmer says his replica will be 56,000, partly to accommodate safety features – and modern luxuries that include a casino. While his plan calls for the new ship to be launched in 2016, it is delayed until 2018, and then delayed again due to problems with financing the $500 million project. Asked if *Titanic II* will be unsinkable, Palmer replies: 'Of course, it will sink if you put a hole in it.'
- **November 2016:** In China, work begins on a stationary replica of the *Titanic* by the Romandisea Seven Star International

Cultural Tourism Resort. The 'ship' will be a museum and hotel, featuring dining halls, theatres, observation decks, cabins and fixtures that replicate the original British liner. A night aboard will cost up to $2,000 Chinese Yuan – or about £235 sterling ($311). The replica is unlikely to suffer the same fate as its namesake, as it will be located in landlocked Daying County, more than 600 miles from the ocean.

- **October 2018:** Following the ruling of a U.S. bankruptcy judge in the case of RMS *Titanic*, the company and its assets – including all artefacts it owns from the doomed ship – are released for sale to the highest bidder. The thousands of artefacts include clothing, letters, cookware, coins, floor tiles, coal and part of the hull of the wrecked ship. The *Titanic* Museum in Belfast attempts to purchase the items, but is unable to raise enough money. RMS *Titanic*'s assets are eventually bought by a group of hedge fund investors for $19.5 million.

- **29 September 2019:** *Britannic* claims one more life as a British diver, Tim Saville, is killed while on a 393-foot-dive to the wreck.

- **January 2020:** *Titanic*, the world's most famous shipwreck, becomes more rigorously protected under an international agreement between the United States and the United Kingdom. Together, the two nations will now be responsible for granting permits to those who plan to visit the wreck and remove artefacts.

- **22 July 2020:** RMS *Titanic*, Inc., says it will attempt to recover the Marconi wireless telegraph equipment from inside *Titanic*, which was used to call for help after the ship struck the iceberg. The announcement follows a decision by a U.S. federal judge overturning a previously issued order from July 2000 to stop anyone cutting into or detaching parts of the ship. In the new ruling, Judge Rebecca Smith, of Virginia's Eastern District Court, writes the salvage of the radio equipment allows a 'unique opportunity to recover an artifact' that would significantly add to the *Titanic*'s legacy.

- **December 2020:** Celebrity chef Prue Leith appears on British TV on *Who Wants To Be A Millionaire?* and misses an opportunity to raise £48,000 for charity when she's asked 'Which of these senior crew members on RMS *Titanic* survived the sinking?' She is offered the following answers: First Officer William Murdoch, Chief designer Thomas Andrews, Second Officer Charles Lightoller or Captain Edward Smith. After phoning a friend and using a 50/50 lifeline, her choices are narrowed to just two: Second Officer Charles Lightoller or Captain Edward Smith. She erroneously chooses Captain Smith as a stunned nation watches.

- **April 2021:** OceanGate Expeditions publishes a brochure offering the sale of research tours of the *Titanic*'s wreck site. The company says its expeditions 'will be conducted respectfully and in accordance with NOAA Guidelines for Research Exploration and Salvage of RMS Titanic and comply with UNESCO guidelines for the preservation of underwater world heritage sites.' The cost per person for research training and a trip to the ship is listed as $250,000. Meanwhile, two other companies, Bluefish and Blue Marble have also promoted trips, but at bargain basement prices – with Blue Marble quoting a price of $105,129 and Bluefish offering trips at just $59,680.

- **May 2021:** Robert Ballard, who discovered the remains of *Titanic* in 1985, releases a book in which he claims the mission to find the wreck was backed by the U.S. Navy in an effort to rattle the Russians psychologically, by making them believe the U.S. had capabilities far beyond their own. In making his pitch for the Navy's support to find the *Titanic*, Ballard says: 'I'll find it, and then we'll go public… show videos from the robots roaming through the ballrooms. It will drive the Soviets crazy. They'll think that if we're willing to publicise this capability, imagine what our Navy is doing in secret.'

- **3 August 2021:** Three people are injured at a *Titanic* museum in Pigeon Forge, Tennessee when an iceberg exhibit falls on them, requiring the trio to be hospitalised. The museum, modelled after the ship, also features a frozen 'iceberg' visitors can touch. After its collapse, the iceberg is cordoned off and takes a month to rebuild.

- **7 October 2021:** Lego announces its largest set to date, 'The Lego Titanic', consisting of 9,090 pieces. When fully built, it measures 53 inches in length and is designed to represent the luxury liner as authentically as possible. In addition, it has three sections that can be opened to showcase its interior features, including the grand staircase, boiler room, smoking lounge, promenade deck, swimming pool, the bridge and working piston engines that turn the propellers. 'The Lego Titanic' also comes with a hefty price to boot: £476.49 ($629.99) – about forty-two times the cost of the cheapest third-class ticket on the original ship's 1912 maiden voyage. Pre-orders of the Lego model immediately sell out and it is backordered.

- **October 2021:** OceanGate Expeditions reports on the deteriorating condition of the *Titanic* after making ten dives to the wreck site over the summer. Researchers document that many areas of the ship have begun to collapse and that some interior spaces are now visible where walls have caved in. They report the starboard areas where the captain's and officers' quarters were located are particularly affected, as is the promenade deck. *Titanic* is quickly becoming a pile of rust.

- **2030:** The year some researchers believe the remains of the *Titanic* will disappear, eaten away by hungry bacteria. In 2010, proteobacteria were found on 'rusticles' recovered from the wreckage. Scientists named the new bacteria 'Halomonas Titanicae' and believe it is likely to completely erode what is left of the wreck. However, the memory of the *Titanic* will remain long after her physical presence has disappeared.

Index